Why You're Creatively Blocked

And The Mellow Mastermind Way to Fix It

Wanda Rogers

Why You're Creatively Blocked And The Mellow Mastermind Way To Fix It

Copyright © 2025 by Wanda Rogers

All rights reserved. No part of this publication may be reproduced, distributed, or transmitted in any form or by any means, including photocopying, recording, or other electronic or mechanical methods, without the prior written permission of the publisher, except in the case of brief quotations embodied in critical reviews and certain other noncommercial uses permitted by copyright law.

For permission requests, write to the author at info@officiallymars.com.

First Edition: September 2025

ISBN: 979-8-9930786-0-1

Publisher: Wanda Rogers

The publisher is not responsible for websites (or their content) that are not owned by the publisher.

Author's Note: The techniques and strategies described in this book are based on research, personal experience, and anecdotal evidence from creative professionals. While every effort has been made to provide accurate and helpful information, results may vary. This book is not intended as a substitute for professional mental health advice. If you're experiencing persistent creative blocks that significantly impact your well-being, please consult with a qualified mental health professional.

Some names and identifying details of individuals mentioned in case studies and examples have been changed to protect privacy.

Disclaimer: The author is not affiliated with, sponsored by, or receiving compensation from any of the tools, apps, or resources mentioned in this publication. All recommendations are based on personal experience, research, and the experiences of trusted creative professionals.

For more resources and to connect with the Mellow Mastermind community, visit @MellowMastermind on Instagram, YouTube, and TikTok, and 'Mellow Mastermind Community Server' on Discord.

Printed in the United States of America

For everyone who's ever stared at a blank page and wondered if they were actually creative at all. Spoiler alert: you are.

DEDICATION

For every creator who has ever:

Opened a document titled "New Project" and immediately closed it again.

Spent three hours organizing their creative workspace instead of actually creating anything.

Wondered if that brilliant idea they had in the shower was actually brilliant, or if shower thoughts are just regular thoughts with better acoustics.

Bought the perfect notebook and then became too afraid to write in it because what if their first idea wasn't perfect or "new notebook" worthy.

Compared their rough draft to someone else's finished masterpiece and decided maybe they should take up another interest instead.

And especially for:

My past self, who spent countless hours researching "how to write something meaningful" instead of just writing something. This book exists because I finally gave myself permission to write badly first.

The creative humans who shared their blocks, fears, and breakthroughs with me — your vulnerability made this book possible, and your courage to create imperfectly makes the world more interesting.

My family, who never once questioned why I needed seventeen different notebooks for the same purpose or why I insisted on sitting in peace in the most obscure positions to "make it happen" for myself... You're the unsung heroes of the freelance creative economy.

And most importantly:

For you, holding this book right now, probably wondering if you should read it or if you should organize your desk first.

Read the book. The desk will still be there when you're done, and honestly, it'll probably still be messy... or however you like to naturally keep it. That's what makes it a creative space instead of a museum.

You don't need to be ready to create. You don't need to be perfect to start. You don't need to have it all figured out to make something meaningful.

You just need to begin.

This book is your permission slip to do exactly that — messily, imperfectly, and with way more self-compassion than you probably think you deserve.

You deserve it. Your ideas deserve it. The world deserves to see what you make when you stop waiting for the perfect moment and start working with the beautifully chaotic moment you're actually in.

Now stop reading dedication pages and go make something. *(After you finish the book, obviously. I mean, I wrote the whole thing... The least you could do is read it. Haha)*

With love, juice, and the firm belief that your creativity is not broken,

Wanda Rogers

EPIGRAPH

"The way to get started is to quit talking and begin doing." — Walt Disney

"You can't use up creativity. The more you use, the more you have." — Maya Angelou

"The secret to getting ahead is getting started." — Mark Twain

"I love deadlines. I love the whooshing noise they make as they go by." — Douglas Adams

"Perfectionism is the voice of the oppressor, the enemy of the people. It will keep you cramped and insane your whole life, and it is the main obstacle between you and a shitty first draft." — Anne Lamott

---

"Your brain isn't broken. The system you've been trying to use is broken." — A note I wrote to myself at 2 AM after spending six hours 'organizing' my creative projects instead of working on them

Table of Contents

Your Brain Isn't Broken	1
The Block Breakdown	7
Steal Like a Pro	23
The 70% Rule	35
The 5-Minute Trick	49
Weaponize Your Environment	63
The Feedback Loop	81
When to Ignore All This Advice	101
The Mellow Mastermind Lifestyle	121
Quick Reference Guide	139
Resources and Tools for the Mellow Mastermind	159
Get To Know the Author	177

Why You're Creatively Blocked

INTRODUCTION

Your Brain Isn't Broken
The Real Truth About Creativity

Let's get one thing straight: if you've ever stared at a blinking cursor like it personally offended you, spiraled into a TikTok binge instead of starting your next big thing, or convinced yourself that maybe you're just not "creative enough," you're not lazy. You're not unmotivated. And no, your brain isn't broken.

You've just been taught creativity wrong.

We've been sold a very seductive, very toxic lie: that creativity is some mystical force that either blesses you or doesn't. The "lightning strike" model where real artists just wait for the Muse™ to descend upon them with inspiration.

Yeah. About that. Science called. It wants to talk...

The Great Creative Lie We've All Been Sold

> The "lightning strike" model of creativity isn't just wrong — it's actively harmful. It sets up this false binary where you're either a "creative person" (touched by divine inspiration) or you're not. It makes creativity feel like a personality trait rather than what it actually is: a skill that can be developed through practice and the right approach.

This myth has its roots in centuries of artistic romanticism, where we've elevated the tortured genius archetype to near-religious status. But here's what those stories conveniently leave out: Van Gogh painted over 2,000 artworks in just over a decade — that's obsessive daily practice. Kerouac rewrote "On the Road" multiple times. Mozart composed with the systematic discipline of a craftsman.

The inspiration myth persists because it's more compelling than the truth. We'd rather believe in magic than confront the unsexy reality of consistent effort.

What Creativity Actually Looks Like (Spoiler: It's Not Pretty)

Here's what happens in creative work: It's messy, iterative, and often boring. Real creativity looks like showing up consistently — even when you don't feel inspired. It looks like generating ten terrible ideas to get to one decent one. It looks like editing, revising, and wrestling with problems until something clicks.

The "aha!" moments exist, but they're usually the result of sustained effort, not divine intervention.

The Paralysis Problem: Why That Cursor Keeps Blinking

The "blinking cursor" paralysis is often perfectionism disguised as creative block. We've been conditioned to think that if the first draft isn't brilliant, we're failing. But first drafts aren't supposed to be brilliant — they're supposed to exist.

Why You're Creatively Blocked

Your brain craves constraints, boundaries, and clear starting points. The cursor blinks because you're trying to solve the entire creative problem at once instead of just solving the first small piece.

Meet the 5 Block Archetypes

Everyone gets creatively blocked. But how do YOU get blocked? That's where things get interesting. Let me introduce you to your new inner frenemies:

> 1. The Overthinker: You create 37 hypothetical versions of your idea in your head… and produce zero in real life. You probably say things like, "But what if it's cringe?"

> 2. The Perfectionist: You edit the first sentence of your novel for 9 weeks straight. Your Canva designs have been optimized but you've posted nothing since 2022

> 3. The Distracted: You're working on your screenplay. Just as soon as you reorganize your Notion dashboard, alphabetize your emails, and check Instagram… for research, of course.

> 4. The Idea-Hopper: You have 47 brilliant concepts and zero finished projects. Every new idea feels more exciting than the one you're currently avoiding.

> 5. **The Burnout:** You used to love creating, but now it feels like another item on your impossible to-do list.

Sound familiar? You'll get to officially diagnose your Block Type in Chapter 1, complete with a quiz and targeted solutions.

The Mellow Mastermind Philosophy

What Is a Mellow Mastermind?

A Mellow Mastermind is someone who gets extraordinary results through strategic ease rather than brute force. They understand that creativity isn't about suffering for your art; it's about creating sustainable systems that honor both your ambition and your humanity.

> The Mellow Mastermind approach is based on five core principles:
>
> 1. **Steal Like a Pro:** You don't need to reinvent the wheel. Just remix it better than anyone else.
> 2. **The 70% Rule:** Done is better than dazzling. Perfect is the enemy of shipped.
> 3. **The 5-Minute Trick:** Start before your brain has a chance to whine about it.
> 4. **Weaponize Your Environment:** Design your life for flow, not force.
> 5. **The Feedback Loop:** Track progress without being a judgmental jerk to yourself.

Why You're Creatively Blocked

This book won't tell you to "hustle harder" or "just believe in yourself." You've had enough of that Pinterest nonsense. Instead, we'll get into brain-based, soul-soothing principles that actually work.

Who This Book Is For

This book is for the poets stuck mid-stanza, the screenwriters with gorgeous Google Docs titled "Idea 1" through "Idea 27," and the burned-out creatives who used to love making things but now feel exhausted by the thought of creating.

You're not broken. You're not lazy. Your creative spark didn't die — it's just buried under layers of perfectionism, comparison, and the crushing weight of infinite possibility.

If you feel like your brain is hosting a never-ending group chat between ADHD, anxiety, and capitalism... then welcome home.

How This Book Works

Each chapter builds on the previous one, creating a complete creative operating system:

- Chapter 1 helps you identify your specific block type
- Chapters 2-6 gives you targeted tools for each common creative challenge
- Chapter 7 teaches you when to ignore all advice and rest instead
- The Lifestyle section shows you how to sustain these practices long-term

You don't have to read this linearly (though it helps). Jump to the chapter that addresses your biggest current challenge, then circle back to build your complete system.

What Makes This Different

Most creative advice falls into two categories: the woo-woo "trust the universe" approach and/or the productivity-bro "hustle until you collapse" method. Both are designed to make you feel guilty about being human.

This book takes a third path: strategic humanity. We're going to work with your brain's actual wiring, honor your real limitations, and build systems that get stronger over time instead of burning you out.

The Permission You've Been Waiting For

You have permission to create badly. You have permission to start before you feel ready. You have permission to treat creativity as a skill rather than a mystical gift. You have permission to work systematically rather than waiting for lightning to strike.

> *Your brain isn't broken. The system you've been using is broken. It's time to upgrade your creative operating system and start making the work you're capable of making.*

The blank page is waiting. Not for inspiration to strike, but for you to begin.

Why You're Creatively Blocked

CHAPTER 1

The Block Breakdown

You Can't Fix What You Won't Name

Let's be painfully and uncomfortably honest for a moment: most creative advice exists in one of two equally useless extremes, and both are designed to make you feel like garbage about yourself.

> ### DO THIS NOW: THE 60-SECOND BLOCK DETECTIVE
>
> Before we go any further, let's figure out what you're actually dealing with. This exercise captures your brain's automatic response before it can put on its "I'm totally fine" mask.
>
> Set a timer for 60 seconds and stream-of-consciousness answer this question:
>
> "What happens in my brain the moment I sit down to do creative work?"
>
> Instructions:
>
> 1. Open your notes app or grab a piece of paper
> 2. Set timer for exactly 60 seconds
> 3. Write continuously - don't stop, don't edit, don't worry about grammar

> 4. If you get stuck, write "I'm stuck" and keep going
> 5. When timer goes off, STOP immediately
>
> Common responses and what they reveal:
>
> - "I immediately think of seventeen other things I should do first" → Distraction pattern
> - "I start questioning whether this idea is even good" → Fear of judgment
> - "I feel overwhelmed by how much work it's going to be" → Perfectionist overwhelm
> - "I get distracted by literally anything else" → Avoidance mechanism
> - "I feel exhausted just thinking about starting" → Burnout indicator
>
> Your raw response is data - keep it for the quiz below.

On one side, you have the mystical, woo-woo approach — the "just follow your heart!" crowd who act like creativity is some ethereal force that only visits the spiritually pure. On the other extreme, you have the productivity-bro brigade — the "wake up at 5am, do cold plunges, and WRITE UNTIL YOU BLEED" enthusiasts who treat creativity like Navy SEAL training.

No thanks to both approaches. We're taking door number three.

The truth is, creativity isn't mystical (though it can feel magical when it's working), and it doesn't require you to become a productivity cyborg. What it requires is something much more radical: honest, unflinching self-awareness about what's happening in your brain when you try to create.

Most of us have been fumbling around in the dark for years, trying to solve problems we can't even properly identify. We know something isn't working, but we can't pinpoint what the actual obstacle is.

> *Your creative challenges aren't character flaws that need to be overcome through sheer force of will. They're data points. Information about how your particular brain processes creative work, what environments support your natural rhythms, and what invisible obstacles have been tripping you up.*

Once you can name what's actually happening — once you can say "Oh, I'm dealing with perfectionism disguised as procrastination" — everything changes. Suddenly, you're not fighting some mysterious creative demon. You're solving a specific, addressable problem with specific, proven solutions.

The 5 Creative Block Triggers

After years of working with creative humans (and being one myself), I've discovered that most creative paralysis boils down to one (or more) of these five psychological landmines. These aren't mysterious creative ailments — they're specific, recognizable patterns that show up in predictable ways. Once you can spot them, you can start to defuse them.

And The Mellow Mastermind Way To Fix It

1. Fear of Judgment

You want to make something, but then your brain starts its' not so helpful commentary: *What if it's cringe? What if people see it and laugh? What if they think I'm pretentious for even trying?*

This fear shows up in sneaky ways. Maybe you spend hours researching before you start. Maybe you workshop your ideas to death. Maybe you start projects but never finish them because finishing means putting them out into the world where they can be judged.

Your brain is trying to protect you from embarrassment and social exclusion. From an evolutionary perspective, this makes perfect sense. But in the modern world, this protective mechanism is working overtime, treating every creative risk like a saber-toothed tiger.

> ***The Block Antidote:*** *Start small and public. Share imperfect work early and often. The judgment you fear rarely materializes, and when it does, it's rarely as devastating as your brain predicts.*

2. Choice Paralysis

You've got 57 unfinished ideas living in various notebooks, apps, and corners of your mind. They're all good ideas. Some of them are great ideas. And that's the problem.

Which one do you choose? What if you pick the wrong one and waste months? What if the idea you don't choose was the one that could have changed your life?

Your brain, faced with too many equally appealing options, does what any reasonable computer would do when overloaded: it freezes. It chooses none.

> *The Block Antidote:* Constraints are your friend. Pick one project and commit to finishing it before you're allowed to start anything new. Use deadlines, timers, and artificial limitations to force decisions.

3. Perfectionism

You tell yourself you just want to "get it right." But perfectionism isn't about having high standards — it's fear wearing a productivity hat. It's the fear of not being good enough, disguised as wanting to be excellent.

This shows up as endless research phases, constant revisions before you've even finished a first draft, waiting for the "perfect" time to start, or needing the "perfect" tools before you can begin.

The cruel irony? Perfectionism doesn't lead to perfect work. It leads to no work.

> *The Block Antidote:* Embrace the 70% rule. Ship when it's good enough, not when it's perfect. Set artificial deadlines and honor them regardless of how "ready" you feel.

4. Distraction Addiction

TikTok, Instagram, Twitter, YouTube, and whatever new app just launched are designed to be irresistible dopamine delivery systems. Your brain craves novelty, and these platforms provide an endless stream of it.

Creative work, on the other hand, is often slow, uncertain, and frustrating. It requires sustained focus, tolerance for ambiguity, and the ability to sit with discomfort.

So, when faced with the choice between immediate gratification of scrolling and delayed gratification of creating, your brain chooses the path of least resistance. Every time.

> **The Block Antidote:** *Create friction between you and your distractions. Use airplane mode, website blockers, or physical separation from devices. Make starting your creative work easier than accessing distractions.*

5. Burnout in Disguise

You think you're blocked, but actually? You're running on empty. Maybe you've been pushing too hard for too long, saying yes to too many things, carrying too much mental load.

Burnout doesn't always look like a dramatic collapse. Sometimes it looks like creative paralysis. Sometimes it looks like having ideas but no energy to execute them.

In this case, rest isn't avoidance — it's medicine. You can't create from an empty well.

> **The Block Antidote:** *Rest isn't a reward — it's a requirement. Take breaks without earning them. Focus on filling the creative well before trying to draw from it.*

The beautiful thing about these five triggers is that they're not permanent conditions. They're temporary states that respond to specific interventions. Once you can identify which one (or which combination) is affecting you, you can start to address it directly instead of just hoping willpower will eventually kick in.

What's Your Block Type?

Forget those personality quizzes that tell you which Disney princess you are based on your tea order. This one actually matters. Answer based on your gut reaction, not what you think you *should* feel.

Creative Block Diagnostic Quiz

Question 1: You have a creative project due next week. Your brain immediately:

A) Starts planning every detail and researching "just to make sure I understand fully" until you've read 47 articles but written zero words.
B) Gets excited about the idea but then starts catastrophizing about all the ways it could go wrong or how it might not meet your standards.
C) Agrees this is important and you'll definitely start tomorrow, right after you reorganize your Spotify playlists and check "just a few" TikToks.

D) Generates sixteen other project ideas that suddenly seem way more interesting and manageable than this one.
E) Feels heavy and tired, like someone just asked you to climb Mount Everest in flip-flops.

Question 2: When you think about sharing your creative work, your dominant feeling is:

A) Anxiety that people will find obvious flaws or problems you didn't think of, so you need to research and plan more first.
B) Terror that it's not polished enough, and people will see you as amateur or unprofessional.
C) Overwhelm at the entire process of putting yourself out there - there are just so many steps and decisions.
D) Confusion about which of your many projects actually represents you best right now.
E) Disconnection, like you're not even sure what you want to say anymore or if anyone would care.

Question 3: Your creative workspace currently looks like:

A) A research station with color-coded notes, multiple planning documents, and approximately zero actual creative output visible.

B) Pinterest-perfect and aesthetically pleasing, but you rarely work there because you don't want to mess up the organization.
C) An archaeological dig site of half-finished projects, good intentions, and items that migrated from other parts of your life.
D) Creative chaos with supplies for seven different projects all mixed together because you can't decide which one to focus on.
E) Abandoned or repurposed for something else. Possibly being used to store laundry or bills.

Question 4: Complete this sentence: "I would create more if only..."

A) "I had a complete understanding of what I was doing and a foolproof plan that accounted for every possible challenge."
B) "I could make it really, really good before anyone saw it - like, professional-level good so no one could criticize it."
C) "I had more time, fewer distractions, and the mental energy to focus on creative work instead of everything else."
D) "I could decide which of my ideas deserves my attention and stop getting excited about new possibilities every week."
E) "I had any energy or enthusiasm left at the end of dealing with everything else in my life."

Question 5: When you get a creative idea, you typically:

A) Immediately start researching everything related to it, making lists of what you'd need to do, and planning out the entire process in detail.
B) Get excited but then start worrying about whether you can execute it well enough and begin thinking about all the ways it could go wrong.
C) Write it down or voice-memo it with full intention of working on it later, then somehow never get around to actually starting.
D) Add it to your ever-growing collection of ideas and feel both excited about the new possibility and guilty about the other ideas you haven't worked on.
E) Feel a brief spark of interest but then remember how exhausted you are and push the idea away before it can disappoint you.

Quiz Scoring & Detailed Results

Count your As, Bs, Cs, Ds, and Es:

Mostly A's = The Overthinker *Primary Issue: Fear of Judgment disguised as thoroughness*

Your Block Profile:

- You analyze until you're paralyzed
- Research becomes sophisticated procrastination
- You believe thorough preparation equals creative success

Why You're Creatively Blocked

- You have 17 tabs open for "research" but zero actual output

Your Personalized Prescription:

- Primary Tool: The 5-Minute Trick (Chapter 4) - start before analysis paralysis kicks in
- Secondary Support: Steal Like a Pro (Chapter 2) - remix existing ideas instead of starting from scratch
- Emergency Protocol: Set timer for 15 minutes, create something deliberately bad

Daily Practice: Every morning, before checking email or doing research, spend 5 minutes creating something related to your project. Anything. Quality doesn't matter.

Mostly B's = The Perfectionist *Primary Issue: Fear of Judgment disguised as high standards*

Your Block Profile:

- You're editing as you create (like driving with the brake on)
- Your standards are impossible because they're designed to avoid criticism
- You spend more time polishing than creating
- Nothing feels "ready" to share

Your Personalized Prescription:

- Primary Tool: The 70% Rule (Chapter 3) - ship when it's good enough, not perfect
- Secondary Support: The Feedback Loop (Chapter 6) - measure progress, not perfection

- Emergency Protocol: Set deadline for TODAY, publish whatever exists when time's up

Daily Practice: Every piece you work on gets a maximum "polish time" - when that's up, you share it regardless of how "ready" it feels.

Mostly C's = The Distracted *Primary Issue: Attention hijacked by digital dopamine*

Your Block Profile:

- You're not lazy, you're overstimulated
- Your nervous system is in constant fight-or-flight from digital inputs
- Creative work feels slow compared to the instant gratification of scrolling
- You lose creative time to "productive" procrastination

Your Personalized Prescription:

- Primary Tool: Weaponize Your Environment (Chapter 5) - design space that eliminates distraction triggers
- Secondary Support: The 5-Minute Trick (Chapter 4) - build focus gradually through micro-commitments
- Emergency Protocol: Phone in airplane mode, work with pen and paper only

Daily Practice: Create a "distraction-free zone" - one specific time and place where devices aren't allowed and creativity happens.

Mostly D's = The Idea-Hopper *Primary Issue: Choice paralysis and commitment avoidance*

Why You're Creatively Blocked

Your Block Profile:

- Your brain is a goldmine of concepts, graveyard of execution
- You're addicted to the excitement of new ideas
- Existing projects feel limited and require actual work
- You have notebooks full of brilliant unfinished concepts

Your Personalized Prescription:

- Primary Tool: The 70% Rule (Chapter 3) - use constraints and deadlines to force completion
- Secondary Support: The Feedback Loop (Chapter 6) - track completion metrics, not idea generation
- Emergency Protocol: Write down ALL ideas, pick ONE, commit to finishing before starting anything new

Daily Practice: "One Project Rule" - work only on your designated project until it's complete enough to share. New ideas go in an "idea parking lot" for later.

Mostly E's = The Burnout *Primary Issue: Creative exhaustion and depletion*

Your Block Profile:

- You're not blocked, you're running on empty
- Creativity feels like obligation, not invitation
- You've been giving more than you have for too long
- The thought of creating feels exhausting, not exciting

Your Personalized Prescription:

- Primary Tool: When to Ignore All Advice (Chapter 7) - rest is required, not earned
- Secondary Support: Weaponize Your Environment (Chapter 5) - create restoration-focused space
- Emergency Protocol: Complete creative break for minimum one week, no guilt allowed

Daily Practice: Before trying to create anything, assess your energy level. If it's below 6/10, rest instead. Creating from depletion produces poor work and deepens burnout.

Mixed Results Interpretation

If your answers were fairly evenly spread: You're dealing with multiple block types, which is completely normal. Most creators have a primary block (highest score) and a secondary pattern (second highest) that shows up under stress.

Your Action Plan:

1. Address your primary block type first for 2 weeks
2. Then integrate tools for your secondary pattern
3. Use Chapter 7 protocols when overwhelmed by multiple blocks

System Integration Note: The beauty of the Mellow Mastermind approach is that these tools work together. Chapter 4's 5-minute starts work with Chapter 3's 70% shipping. Chapter 5's environment design supports all other techniques. Chapter 6's feedback helps you understand which combinations work best for your brain.

DO THIS NOW: THE CREATIVE BLOCK NAME GAME

This might seem silly, but humor is one of the most powerful tools we have for disarming fear. When you can laugh at something, it loses its grip on you.

Step 1: Take your block type from the quiz above.

Step 2: Give it a ridiculous, affectionate nickname that makes you smile. Think less "my crippling perfectionism" and more "my overzealous quality control manager."

Examples to spark your creativity:

- The Overthinker becomes "Professor Research Rabbit Hole" or "Dr. What-If Scenarios"
- The Perfectionist becomes "Captain Never-Good-Enough" or "The Supreme Nitpicker"
- The Distracted becomes "Admiral Squirrel Brain" or "The Notification Detective"
- The Idea-Hopper becomes "The Butterfly Collector" or "Professor Shiny-New-Thing"
- The Burnout becomes "The Empty Battery" or "Captain Running-on-Fumes"

Step 3: Practice your new response. Next time your block shows up, try: "Oh look, Professor Research Rabbit Hole is back. Thanks for trying to keep me safe, Prof, but I'm going to start writing now."

Why this works: When you're in the grip of a creative block, it feels huge and completely true. But when you

> give it a silly name and talk to it like a quirky character, you create psychological distance. You become an observer of your patterns instead of being trapped inside them.
>
> What you can name, you can manage.

Your creative blocks aren't enemies — they're just outdated protective mechanisms that need some gentle management. And sometimes, the best management tool is a good laugh.

What you can name, you can understand. What you can understand, you can work with. What you can work with, you can transform.

Why You're Creatively Blocked
CHAPTER 2

Steal Like a Pro
Originality is a Myth, Remixing is an Art

Here's a hot take to start off your Tuesday afternoon identity crisis: Nothing you make is truly original. And that's not just okay — it's liberating.

> **DO THIS NOW: THE CREATIVE DNA MAPPING EXERCISE**
>
> Before we learn to steal like a pro, let's identify your existing influences so you can remix them consciously instead of unconsciously copying.
>
> Time needed: 15 minutes
>
> Step 1: Current Obsessions Audit (5 minutes) Write down:
>
> - 3 creators you follow religiously
> - 3 shows/movies you've rewatched recently
> - 3 books/articles that made you think "I wish I'd written this"
> - 3 songs that give you creative energy
> - 3 random things you've googled lately out of curiosity

> **Step 2: Voice Recognition (5 minutes)** Answer quickly, don't overthink:
>
> - Who do you sound like when you're explaining something you're passionate about?
> - What phrases do you overuse?
> - Whose writing style do you find yourself mimicking?
> - What tone feels most natural when you create?
>
> **Step 3: Aspiration Identification (5 minutes)** Complete these sentences:
>
> - "I want my work to make people feel..."
> - "The last thing that made me think 'how did they DO that?' was..."
> - "If I could collaborate with anyone, living or dead, it would be..."
> - "The creative work I'm most jealous of is..."
>
> Your Results = Your Remix Recipe

You are a walking, breathing mixtape of everything you've ever consumed. That poem you wrote? It's your grandmother's wisdom mixed with a Chris Brown lyric, shaped by a 3 AM Reddit thread, and topped with your own emotional baggage. That business idea? It's Airbnb meets your college dorm experience meets that frustration you had last week.

So, stop trying to create from scratch like some tortured genius in a Wi-Fi-free cabin. You're not inventing — you're remixing. And the sooner you embrace that, the faster you'll unlock your most effortless ideas.

The Originality Prison (And Why We're Breaking Out)

We've been sold a lie about creativity that's basically creative kryptonite. The myth goes like this: Real artists pull ideas from thin air, channeling pure inspiration through divine Wi-Fi. They sit in empty rooms, staring at blank canvases until lightning strikes. They never reference, never borrow, never build on what came before.

> *This myth is why you're stuck.*

Every minute you spend trying to be "completely original" is a minute you're not creating. You're paralyzed by an impossible standard that literally no human in history has ever achieved. Even the most "original" creators were professional borrowers:

- The Beatles started as a cover band (yes, really)
- Shakespeare lifted plots constantly — "Romeo and Juliet" is basically Italian fanfiction
- Steve Jobs built Apple by remixing existing technologies
- Your favorite TikTok creator is remixing sounds, formats, and trends daily

> *The difference between amateur borrowers and professional remixers isn't whether they borrow — it's how skillfully they transform what they take.*

The Professional Remixer's Toolkit

Here's what separates random copying from strategic borrowing: intentionality. Professional remixers don't just grab whatever's nearby — they curate influences like they're building the perfect playlist.

The Borrowing Hierarchy (What to Steal and How)

Level 1: Steal the Structure *(Safest and most effective)*

- How they organized their argument
- The way they paced their reveal
- Their method for building tension
- The format they used to present information

Level 2: Steal the Style *(Medium risk, high reward)*

- Their tone of voice
- How they transition between ideas
- Their approach to humor or seriousness
- The way they connect with their audience

Level 3: Steal the Surface *(Highest risk, often lazy)*

- Specific phrases or terminology
- Visual aesthetics without understanding
- Direct content copying
- Following trends without adding perspective

The pros live in Levels 1 and 2. The amateurs get stuck in Level 3.

The Ethics of Creative Borrowing

Before we dive into the how-to, let's address the elephant in the room: What's the difference between inspiration and appropriation?

Smart borrowing follows three key principles:

Credit When Possible: When your remix is clearly inspired by someone specific, acknowledge it. "Inspired by [creator]" or "In the style of [influence]" goes a long way.

Transform, Don't Copy: You're borrowing structure, style, or approach - not copying content word-for-word or image-for-image.

Punch Up, Not Down: Be especially thoughtful when borrowing from smaller creators or marginalized communities. Ask: "Am I amplifying or overshadowing?"

When in doubt, reach out. Most creators are flattered when you ask permission or give attribution. The worst they can say is no.

The Remix Method: Your 3-Step Creative Alchemy

Step 1: Curate (Don't Just Consume)

Stop consuming content like a zombie scrolling for dopamine hits. Start hunting like a curator building an exhibition.

Create Your Influence Archive:

- Hooks that stopped me while scrolling — opening lines that grabbed your attention
- Structures that just worked — how they organized information or told their story
- Voices I want to learn from — tones and personalities that resonate
- Transitions that felt smooth — how they moved between ideas seamlessly
- Endings that hit different — conclusions that stuck with you

The Curation Test: If something makes you feel anything — jealousy, excitement, "dang, I wish I'd thought of that" — capture it immediately. Your emotional response is data about what works.

Step 2: Transform (Add Your Secret Sauce)

This is where the magic happens. You're not copying — you're translating. You're asking: "What would this look like if it came from MY brain, with MY experiences, for MY people?"

The Transformation Techniques:

Medium Switch: Take a Twitter thread structure and turn it into a podcast episode. Take a TikTok format and stretch it into a blog post. The constraint shift forces innovation.

Context Flip: Take a business framework and apply it to dating. Take a cooking show format and use it to teach photography. Take therapy techniques and apply them to creative blocks.

Tone Translation: Take something academic and make it conversational. Take something serious and add humor. Take something corporate and make it personal.

Personal Filter: Add your obsessions, your cultural background, your weird knowledge, your specific problems. That's where your voice lives.

Genre Blend: Mix unexpected influences. What if Marie Groover met marketing strategy? What if true crime podcasts met productivity advice?

Step 3: Ship (Before You Can Talk Yourself Out of It)

Here's where 90% of would-be remixers stall. You've created something inspired by something else, and now your brain is like: "But what if people notice? What if they think I'm a fraud? What if the original creator sees this?"

Here's the truth: They want you to be influenced by them. Influence is the highest form of flattery. When you remix someone's work thoughtfully, you're not stealing from them — you're building on their foundation.

Your Shipping Process:

1. Credit when possible - "Inspired by [original creator]" goes a long way
2. Add clear value - What new perspective/insight does your remix contribute?

And The Mellow Mastermind Way To Fix It

3. Ship at 70% - Don't wait for perfect, just wait for yours
4. Gather feedback - Real responses beat imaginary criticism every time

---

DO THIS NOW: THE WIKIPEDIA REMIX CHALLENGE

Time for some creative cross-training. This exercise will stretch your remixing muscles in the weirdest, most effective way possible.

Time needed: 10 minutes total

This exercise builds your "remix muscle" by forcing you to find creative gold in completely random material.

The Complete Protocol:

Step 1: The Random Landing (1 minute)

- Go to https://en.wikipedia.org/wiki/Special:Random
- Click once - NO refreshing for a "better" topic
- Scan the page for exactly 1 minute
- Pick ONE sentence that sparks anything (curiosity, confusion, amusement)

Step 2: The Creative Translation (8 minutes) Transform that sentence into content for YOUR medium:

- Writers: Turn it into a poem, story opening, or metaphor

- Visual artists: Create a concept, color palette, or composition idea
- Musicians: Find rhythm, mood, or lyrical inspiration
- Entrepreneurs: Extract a business lesson or market insight
- Content creators: Make it a social media post, video concept, or newsletter topic

Step 3: The Courage Challenge (1 minute) Share it somewhere - text to a friend, post on social media, add to your creative portfolio. Tag it with #WikipediaRemix and #MellowMastermind if you're feeling bold.

Example Transformations: *Wikipedia:* "The mantis shrimp can see twelve types of color receptors (humans only have three)."

Possible Remixes:

- Poem: "What colors am I missing? / What spectrums lie beyond / my three-note vision?"
- Business insight: "We all have perceptual limitations. What is your industry's 'mantis shrimp' seeing that you're missing?"
- Song concept: A melody about seeing the world through different eyes
- Visual art: A series showing the same scene through different "color receptors"

Why This Works:

- Breaks perfectionism: You can't be precautious about random Wikipedia content
- Trains pattern recognition: Your brain learns to find inspiration anywhere
- Practices constraints: Time limit forces action over deliberation
- Builds shipping courage: Low stakes make sharing easier

Real Talk: Learning from the Masters

Let's do a little art history flex:

- Picasso famously said, "good artists copy, great artists steal." He "borrowed" stylistic cues from African sculptures and masks — elements that heavily influenced Cubism. Was it respectful? Debatable. Was it foundational? Absolutely.
- Duchamp took a literal urinal, flipped it upside down, called it "*Fountain*", and submitted it to an art show. It changed modern art forever.

Neither of these creators waited for their own "pure" idea. They hijacked something already out in the world and reframed it.

Modern equivalent? Taking a viral TikTok trend and flipping it into a poem about heartbreak in 200 characters. Remix culture is the culture now.

Pro Tip: Stop Waiting to Be Unique

Here's the trap: "Everyone's already done this. I need to do something no one's seen before."

Wrong! No one's done it like you. With your upbringing. Your slang. Your scars. Your sense of humor. Your quiet rage. Your weird uniqueness.

> *Your job isn't to invent something new. It's to make the familiar feel fresh.*

Your Unavoidable Uniqueness You are the only person who has lived your exact combination of experiences. That combination is your creative signature, whether you realize it or not.

The Specificity Superpower The more specific you get about your own weird experiences, the more universal your work becomes. When you write about growing up as the only vegetarian in a house of BBQ enthusiasts, you're not just writing for other vegetarians — you're writing for anyone who's ever felt different from their family.

The Permission Slip You Didn't Know You Needed

Here's your official permission to be influenced:

- Permission to love other people's work and want to create your own version
- Permission to start with someone else's structure and make it your own

And The Mellow Mastermind Way To Fix It

- Permission to combine influences in ways that feel natural to you
- Permission to build on existing ideas instead of inventing everything from scratch
- Permission to be obvious about your influences instead of hiding them.

The world doesn't need you to invent fire. It needs you to decide what you want to light up.

Stop waiting for lightning bolt inspiration. Start with what already exists and ask: "How would I do this?" Then actually do it.

Your remixes are waiting. Time to start mixing.

Remember: You don't need to be completely original. You need to be courageously yourself while building on what came before you. That's not cheating — that's how culture evolves.

Why You're Creatively Blocked
CHAPTER 3

The 70% Rule
Why Perfection is Creative Kryptonite

Perfection is the enemy of progress. And honestly, it's exhausting.

You've probably been told to "give 110%" your whole life. But here's the thing: 110% is a mathematical impossibility and a psychological trap. Your time, energy, and creative juice are finite resources. And when you chase perfection, you're usually just procrastinating in a more socially acceptable outfit.

> **DO THIS NOW: THE PERFECTIONIST REALITY CHECK**
>
> Before we dive into the 70% rule, let's get honest about what perfectionism is actually costing you.
>
> Grab your phone and quickly answer these:
>
> 1. Name one project you've been "perfecting" for more than a month. What specifically are you still tweaking?
> 2. What would happen if you published it exactly as it is right now? (Write down the actual worst-case scenario, not your anxiety's horror movie version)

> 3. What has not shipping it cost you so far? (Opportunities missed, feedback not received, people not helped)
>
> Keep these answers handy. We're going to come back to them.

The sweet spot for creative momentum? Seventy percent. Not polished. Not flawless. Just good enough to ship and learn from.

Let me guess what just happened in your brain: "But what if people think it's not good enough? What if I could make it better with just a little more time? What if this represents my work and it's not my best?"

I see you, perfectionist. I used to be you. Let me tell you how and why 70% changes everything.

The Perfectionist's Prison (And Why the Door Was Never Locked)

Picture this: You're staring at a project that's pretty dang good. Not perfect, but solid. Helpful. Ready to help someone else. But instead of sharing it, you start the familiar spiral:

"Maybe I should add one more example... Actually, this section could be clearer... Oh man, what if there's a typo? What if people think I don't know what I'm talking about?

Meanwhile, that project sits in your drafts folder, slowly suffocating under the weight of your impossible standards. And while you're perfecting paragraph three for the seventeenth time, someone else ships a "worse" version of a similar idea and gets all the credit, engagement, and feedback that could have been yours.

> *Here's the brutal truth:* ***Perfectionism isn't about high standards. It's about fear wearing a productivity mask.***

The Mathematics of Diminishing Returns (Or: Why That Last 30% Stresses You Out)

Here's what every perfectionist learns the hard way: the journey from 70% to 100% often takes longer than the journey from 0% to 70%.

Think about it:

0-70%: Building the core, solving the main problem, creating the primary value

70-100%: Tweaking fonts, second-guessing word choices, adding "just one more thing," fixing things that weren't actually broken

That final 30% is where projects go to die. It's where good ideas become perfect ideas that never see the light of day.

Meanwhile, the person who ships at 70% is already three projects ahead, learning from real feedback instead of imaginary criticism. They're building momentum, reputation, and actual skills while you're building anxiety.

What 70% Actually Looks Like (The Reality Check)

Let's calibrate what we mean by 70%, because it's not about being sloppy or lazy. It's about being strategic with your perfectionism.

70% Writing Means:

- ✅ The main idea is clearly communicated
- ✅ The structure makes logical sense
- ✅ It would genuinely help someone
- ✅ There are no major factual errors
- ✅ The tone matches your intention
- ❌ Every sentence isn't poetry
- ❌ You haven't explored every possible angle
- ❌ The conclusion isn't earth-shattering

70% Visual Content Means:

- ✅ The message is clear and readable
- ✅ The composition serves the content
- ✅ It represents your authentic style
- ✅ Technical quality doesn't interfere with understanding

❌ The lighting isn't magazine-perfect

❌ Every element isn't precisely aligned

❌ The color palette isn't flawless

70% Video/Audio Means:

✅ Content is audible and visible

✅ Main points come across clearly

✅ Pacing allows for comprehension

✅ Energy matches the message

❌ Audio isn't studio-quality

❌ There are no "ums" or awkward pauses

❌ Every transition is seamless

> ***The key insight:*** *70% serves its purpose. 100% serves your ego.*

DO THIS NOW: THE 70% AUDIT

Look at something you're currently working on. Honestly assess:

1. Does it solve the problem it set out to solve?
2. Would it be helpful to someone right now?
3. Does it represent your authentic voice/style?

> 4. What specific things are you still "fixing"?
>
> If you answered yes to the first three questions, you're probably at 70%. Those things you're still fixing? That's the perfectionist tax you're paying.

The Feedback Revolution: Why Real Beats Imaginary

At 70%, something magical happens: you get actual feedback instead of the fictional feedback you've been getting from shower conversations with yourself.

Real people tell you real things about your real work. And here's the kicker — their feedback is usually about stuff you never even considered, not the tiny details you've been obsessing over.

Things you worry about:

- Whether that one sentence is too casual
- If the color scheme is cohesive enough
- Whether you explained that concept clearly
- If the pacing feels right

Things people actually comment on:

- "This helped me solve a problem I've had for months"
- "I wish you'd talked more about X"
- "Can you do a follow-up about Y?"
- "Where can I learn more about this?"

They're not dissecting your font choices. They're engaging with your ideas. But you'll never know what resonates if you never hit publish.

The Platform-Specific 70% Strategy Guide

Different platforms have different tolerance levels for imperfection. Here's how to calibrate your 70% for each:

Instagram: The "Authentically Imperfect" Paradise: Audiences increasingly prefer "real" content over polished perfection. Good lighting and clear subject matter are important, but don't stress about professional photography.

TikTok: The Raw Energy Champion: Audiences reward authenticity and personality over production value. Phone camera is fine, focus on good enough audio and genuine reactions.

LinkedIn: The "Professional Work-in-Progress" Platform: Audiences appreciate transparency about growth and learning. Share insights you're developing, not just conclusions you've reached.

YouTube: The Long-Form Learning Lab: Good audio is crucial, but visuals can be simple. Complete thoughts and actionable takeaways matter more than perfect delivery.

Email/Newsletter: The Intimate Connection: Conversational and helpful beats formal and comprehensive. Clean and readable beats beautiful and complex.

> **DO THIS NOW: THE 10-SECOND SHIP DECISION**
>
> Here's your new publishing protocol. When you're debating whether something is "ready," set a timer for 10 seconds and ask:
>
> 1. Does this help someone? (Yes/No)
> 2. Is it honestly my best available effort right now? (Yes/No)
> 3. Will waiting another week actually improve it significantly? (Yes/No)
>
> If you answered Yes, Yes, No — hit publish when the timer goes off. Don't think during the countdown, just act.
>
> This isn't about lowering your standards. It's about raising your shipping frequency.

The Perfectionist Panic Protocol

Right before you hit publish, your perfectionist brain will stage its final revolt. Here's your step-by-step protocol for moving through the resistance:

Step 1: Name the Fear "I notice I'm feeling scared about publishing this. What specifically am I afraid of?"

Step 2: Cost-Benefit Analysis Cost of publishing at 70%: Potential minor criticism or feedback; Cost of not publishing: Missed connections, no feedback, no momentum, no impact.

Step 3: The Worst-Case Reality Check Write down the actual worst thing that could happen if you publish this. Usually it's something like: "A few people might not love it" or "Someone might point out something I missed."

Step 4: Publish and Walk Away Hit publish, then immediately do something physical. Go for a walk, make tea, do jumping jacks. Don't check responses for at least an hour.

When 70% Goes Wrong (Spoiler: It Usually Doesn't)

Let's address the elephant in the room: what if your 70% effort flops?

First, let's redefine "flop." A true flop would be publishing something that actively harms people or damages important relationships. Most of what we fear as "flopping" is actually just... normal. Most content gets modest engagement. Most projects have room for improvement.

When a 70% effort gets a lukewarm response:

☑ You learn what resonates (and what doesn't) with your actual audience

☑ You build resilience and realize the world doesn't end when something isn't perfect

☑ You practice your craft — every published piece is training

☑ You maintain momentum — shipping regularly keeps you in creative motion

✅ You gather data for making the next thing better

Success stories from "flops":

- That "rough" blog post that generated three client inquiries
- That "imperfect" video that someone watched during a difficult time
- That "not-quite-ready" course that helped someone change careers
- That "just okay" song that became someone's favorite

You can't predict what will resonate. The only way to find out is to ship it.

DO THIS NOW: THE 70% CHALLENGE

Time to put this into practice. Right now, today, I want you to:

1. Pick something you've been "perfecting" for more than two weeks
2. Assess it honestly — does it serve its core purpose?
3. If yes, ship it within the next 4 hours (seriously, set a timer)
4. If no, give yourself exactly 2 hours to get it to functional, then ship it

Examples of what this might look like:

- That blog post you've rewritten six times → Publish it
- That design you keep tweaking → Send it to the client
- That video you filmed three times → Upload it

- That song you've been mixing forever → Share it
- That business idea you're still "researching" → Create a simple landing page

Don't warn people it's not perfect. Don't apologize for the quality. Just share it like you would any other day.

The Compound Effect of Strategic Imperfection

Here's what happens when you make 70% your new standard:

Month 1: You start shipping more consistently and gathering real feedback. Month 3: You've created more content than in the previous year combined. Month 6: People start commenting on your consistency and productivity. Month 12: You've built a body of work, a reputation, and most importantly, you've trained your perfectionist brain to chill out.

The creators who last aren't the most talented — they're the ones who figured out how to ship regularly without having a nervous breakdown.

Advanced 70% Strategies

Once you're comfortable with basic 70% shipping, here are some advanced tactics:

The Iterative Release Instead of trying to create one perfect piece, create a series:

- "Part 1: The basics of X"

- "Part 2: Advanced X techniques"
- "Part 3: Common X mistakes"

Each piece can be 70% because together they're comprehensive.

The "Learning in Public" Approach Share your work as you develop it:

- "Here's what I'm learning about X"
- "My current thinking on Y (likely to evolve)"
- "Experimenting with Z — here's what I'm finding"

This removes the pressure for each piece to be definitive.

The Beta Version Method Explicitly label things as beta versions:

- "Beta version of my new framework"
- "Testing out this new format"
- "Work in progress, but wanted to share"

This sets appropriate expectations while still providing value.

Remember: The world needs your 70%. It's infinitely better than your 0%.

Stop waiting for perfect. Start shipping good enough. Your future self — the one who actually built something instead of just planning it — will thank you.

Perfect is not the goal. Progress is the goal. Connection is the goal. Impact is the goal.

Why You're Creatively Blocked

The world needs your 70%. Start there.

And The Mellow Mastermind Way To Fix It

Why You're Creatively Blocked
CHAPTER 4

The 5-Minute Trick
Start Before Your Brain Notices

> **DO THIS NOW: THE RESISTANCE RADAR CHECK**
>
> Before we learn to outsmart your brain's resistance, let's identify how your specific brain tries to stop you from creating.
>
> Set a timer for 2 minutes and write down every excuse/distraction/reason your brain offers when you try to start creative work. Don't edit, just dump:
>
> Examples:
>
> - "I should clean my space first"
> - "I need to research this more"
> - "I should check email quickly"
> - "Maybe I should wait until I have more time"
> - "I need the right tools/setup first"
> - "I should plan this out better"
>
> This isn't self-criticism — it's intelligence gathering. You need to know your brain's favorite diversion tactics so you can recognize them in real time.

The Great Creative Heist

Have you ever sat down to start your creative thing — writing, painting, finally organizing that chaotic workspace — and somehow... end up deep-cleaning your bathroom instead? Or falling down a Wikipedia rabbit hole about the mating habits of seahorses? (They're monogamous and the males get pregnant. You're welcome.)

Yeah. That's not you being lazy. That's your brain being a well-meaning but overprotective helicopter parent.

Your brain is basically a security guard who thinks creative work is dangerous. The moment you think "I should write that thing" or "I'll work on my art," your neural alarm system kicks in: *"ALERT! CREATIVE VULNERABILITY DETECTED! INITIATE DISTRACTION PROTOCOL!"*

Suddenly, those baseboards desperately need cleaning. That junk drawer requires immediate organization. You absolutely must research whether pineapple on pizza is actually illegal in Italy (it's not, and pineapples should not go on pizza, but the debate continues).

Here's the thing your brain doesn't want you to know: it's not trying to sabotage you. It's trying to protect you from the three things creative work guarantees:

1. Uncertainty (What if this sucks?)
2. Vulnerability (What if people see the real me?)
3. Effort (What if this is actually hard?)

So, your brain, in its infinite protective wisdom, offers you the sweet relief of productive procrastination. It feels like progress without the scary unknown of creation.

Enter the 5-Minute Trick: Creative Espionage

The 5-Minute Trick is basically creative espionage. You're going to sneak past your brain's security system by being so small, so quick, so seemingly insignificant that the alarm bells never go off.

> *Here's the entire strategy: Start tiny. Start quickly. Start before your brain has time to talk you out of it.*

No grand announcements. No "Today I begin my masterpiece!" declarations. No setting up the perfect creative environment with the right lighting, the perfect playlist, and color-coordinated supplies.

Just... start. For at least five minutes. That's it.

Why Your Brain Hijacks Your Creativity (The Science Made Simple)

Your brain runs on something called a "threat detection system" that evolved when our biggest problems were saber-toothed tigers, not creative blocks. This system can't tell the difference between physical danger and emotional vulnerability.

When you sit down to create something, your brain interprets the potential for judgment, failure, or imperfection as a genuine threat. So, it floods your system with stress hormones and offers you literally anything else to do.

The Creative Threat Assessment:

- Physical danger: Tiger approaching → Fight, flight, or freeze
- Creative vulnerability: Blank page → "Oh look, dishes need washing!"

Your brain would rather have you organize your sock drawer than risk putting your inner world on display. It's not personal — it's biological.

But here's the hack: your threat detection system has a threshold. Small, non-threatening actions fly under the radar. Five minutes feels so manageable that your security system doesn't even wake up.

The Psychology of Micro-Commitments

Five minutes is magical because it hits the sweet spot between "too small to matter" and "big enough to build momentum."

Why 5 minutes works:

- It's non-threatening — Your brain doesn't consider it worth resisting
- It's immediately achievable — You can see the end from the beginning
- It bypasses decision fatigue — No complex choices, just "start the timer"

Why You're Creatively Blocked

- It creates momentum — Moving objects tend to stay in motion (thanks, physics)
- It builds identity — You become someone who shows up, even briefly

Think about it: You've never sat down to write for five minutes and stopped exactly at the five-minute mark because you were bored. You stop because you run out of time, or you hit a natural break, or you realize you've been writing for 45 minutes and your tea is cold.

The hardest part isn't doing the work — it's starting the work. Five minutes gets you over that activation energy hump.

DO THIS NOW: THE 5-MINUTE EXPERIMENT

Right now, before you keep reading, I want you to try it.

Pick any creative project you've been avoiding. Set a timer for 5 minutes and do literally anything related to it:

- Open the document and write one sentence
- Sketch one shape related to your idea
- Record a 30-second voice memo about your concept
- Take one photo for your project
- Write down three words that describe your vision

Don't prepare. Don't plan. Don't wait for the perfect moment. Just start the timer and move.

> Your brain is going to throw a tiny tantrum: "But we should organize first!" "We need more information!" "This isn't the right time!"
>
> Ignore it. You're bigger than your resistance.

Did you do it? Seriously, did you actually do it, or did you just keep reading? If you kept reading, that's your resistance in action. Go back and actually do the 5-minute experiment. I'll wait.

The 5-Minute Variations Menu

The beauty of this trick is that it's infinitely adaptable. Here are variations for different moods, energy levels, and types of creative resistance:

When You're Completely Stuck: The "Anything Counts" Version:

Set 5 minutes and do literally anything project-related:

- Read one paragraph of research
- Organize one folder of materials
- Send one email about the project
- Write three random words related to your idea
- Look at one inspiring example

When You're Overwhelmed: The "One Tiny Thing" Version:

Pick the smallest possible next step:

- Write one sentence

- Sketch one line
- Record one thought
- Take one photo
- Make one decision

When You're Tired: The "Prep for Tomorrow" Version:

Use 5 minutes to set up future you for success:

- Open the documents you'll need
- Gather your materials in one place
- Write yourself a note about what to start with
- Clear your workspace
- Set intentions for tomorrow

When You're Anxious: The "Permission to Suck" Version:

Explicitly create something terrible:

- Write the worst possible opening line
- Make the ugliest sketch
- Record the most awkward voice memo
- Take the most boring photo
- Create the most obvious idea

Permission to suck is permission to start.

When You Have Energy: The "See How Far I Get" Version:

Start with 5 minutes but give yourself permission to continue:

- Set the timer but don't stop if you're in flow
- Use it as a warm-up for a longer session

- Chain multiple 5-minute blocks together
- Let curiosity drive how long you work

DO THIS NOW: DESIGN YOUR PERSONAL 5-MINUTE KIT

Based on your creative work, design your go-to 5-minute starter kit:

1. Your default 5-minute action (the thing you'll do when stuck): _____
2. Your backup action (when the default feels too hard): _____
3. Your materials (what you need within arm's reach): _____
4. Your environment (where you'll do this): _____
5. Your reward (how you'll celebrate showing up): _____

Write this down somewhere you'll see it. When resistance hits, you don't want to have to decide what to do — you want to just execute the plan.

Case Study: Hemingway's "Stop Mid-Sentence" Hack

Ernest Hemingway had a writing habit that seemed completely backwards: he never stopped writing when he ran out of ideas or hit a natural break. Instead, he stopped mid-sentence — on purpose.

His logic was brilliant: The hardest part of writing isn't writing — it's starting to write.

Why You're Creatively Blocked

When you face a blank page, your brain has to make a thousand micro-decisions: What should the first sentence be? What tone? Where should I start? Your decision-fatigued brain looks at all those choices and just... nopes out.

But when you wake up to half a sentence — "Robert Jordan lay behind the pine tree and..." — your brain only has to make one decision: finish the thought.

The Hemingway Principle for Any Creative Work:

- Writers: Stop mid-sentence, mid-paragraph, or mid-thought
- Artists: Leave a sketch half-finished with the next color ready
- Musicians: Stop mid-melody with the next chord progression noted
- Entrepreneurs: End with tomorrow's first task clearly defined

Always leave yourself the easiest possible starting point for next time.

When 5 Minutes Doesn't Work (The Troubleshooting Guide)

Sometimes your resistance is stronger than the 5-minute trick. Here's your troubleshooting protocol:

If You Can't Even Start the Timer: Try: The 1-minute trick, or even 30 seconds; Or: Just gathering your materials without committing to work; Or: Reading about your topic for 5 minutes instead of creating

And The Mellow Mastermind Way To Fix It

If You Stop Exactly at 5 Minutes Every Time: Try: Chain method: set another 5-minute timer immediately; Or: Switch to a different aspect of the project; Or: Lower the stakes even further — maybe you're still aiming too high

If You Keep Getting Distracted: Try: Phone in airplane mode, physical timer instead of phone timer; Or: Work somewhere without Wi-Fi or distractions; Or: Use the "noting" technique: when your mind wanders, just note "thinking" and return to work

If It Feels Pointless: Remember: You're not trying to accomplish everything in 5 minutes. You're trying to prove to your brain that starting is safe. Every 5-minute session is evidence that you're someone who shows up.

DO THIS NOW: THE 5-MINUTE STREAK CHALLENGE

Here's your assignment for the next 7 days:

Day 1-3: Do one 5-minute creative session daily. Any time, any project, any level of quality. Day 4-5: If you missed a day, restart. If you're on track, keep going. Day 6-7: Notice what patterns emerge. What time works best? What type of 5-minute work feels most natural?

Track it simply:

- ✅ Day 1: 5 min writing
- ✅ Day 2: 5 min sketching

> **Day 3:** 5 min planning
>
> The goal isn't perfection — it's data. You're learning how your creative brain actually works in the real world, not in theory.

The Compound Effect of Tiny Starts

Here's what happens when you make 5-minute sessions a habit:

Week 1: You prove to yourself that starting is possible. **Month 1:** You've created more than in the previous 6 months combined. **Month 3:** People start commenting on your consistency and output. **Month 6:** You realize you no longer need the timer — starting has become natural. **Year 1:** You look back and barely recognize the person who used to procrastinate for weeks.

Each 5-minute session is a vote for the identity you want: someone who creates, someone who shows up, someone who turns ideas into reality instead of just collecting them.

Advanced 5-Minute Strategies

Once you're comfortable with basic 5-minute sessions, here are some advanced applications:

The Creative Warm-Up Use 5 minutes to warm up before longer creative sessions:

- 5 minutes of morning pages before "real" writing
- 5 minutes of gesture drawing before detailed artwork
- 5 minutes of improvisation before structured practice

The Problem Solver When stuck on a specific creative problem:

- 5 minutes of brainstorming solutions (quantity over quality)
- 5 minutes of researching how others solved similar problems
- 5 minutes of trying the most obvious solution

The Inspiration Hunter When feeling creatively dry:

- 5 minutes of browsing work you admire
- 5 minutes in nature without devices
- 5 minutes reading something completely unrelated to your field

The Skill Builder For developing craft:

- 5 minutes of practicing one specific technique
- 5 minutes of studying one aspect of someone else's work
- 5 minutes of experimenting with a new tool or approach

The Social Proof Element Want to supercharge your 5-minute practice? Share it. Post a photo of your workspace, blog about your session, text a friend about what you accomplished. You don't have to share the work itself — just the fact that you did the work.

Why You're Creatively Blocked

Remember: The hardest part of any creative work isn't always the middle or the end — It's usually the beginning. The 5-minute trick gets you past that initial resistance and into the flow where creativity actually lives.

Your future creative self is already thanking you for learning to start small.

Stop overthinking. Start the timer. Five minutes is all you need to prove that you're someone who shows up for their ideas.

The blank page is waiting. Not for perfection — just for you to begin.

And The Mellow Mastermind Way To Fix It

Why You're Creatively Blocked
CHAPTER 5

Weaponize Your Environment
Your Space Shapes Your Success

Your space is either working for you or working against you. There's no neutral.

> **DO THIS NOW: THE 30-SECOND SPACE SCAN**
>
> Right now, before reading further, look around your current creative space and count:
>
> - Items within arm's reach that help creativity: ___
> - Items within arm's reach that distract from creativity: ___
> - Seconds it would take to start creating right now: ___
> - Number of steps between deciding to create and actually starting: ___
>
> This isn't judgment — it's data about what we're working with.

Here's a truth that most productivity gurus won't tell you: You could have the most brilliant ideas in the world, but if your environment is designed like a creativity graveyard, those ideas will stay buried next to your good intentions and that novel you swear you'll finish "when you have more time."

Your environment isn't just the backdrop to your creative life — it's an active participant. Every object in your space is either whispering "yes, let's create" or "nah, maybe I should just scroll through social media instead."

The Psychology of Space: Why Your Environment Owns You

When your environment is chaotic, your brain has to work overtime just to filter out distractions. It's like trying to have a deep conversation at a heavy metal concert. Technically possible, but why would you do that to yourself?

But here's where it gets interesting: your brain doesn't just respond to clutter. It responds to **cues**. Those visual reminders scattered around your space are constantly sending signals about what you should be doing:

- Guitar in the corner → "Play me"
- Stack of books → "Read me"
- Pile of unopened mail → "Stress about me"
- Phone face-up on desk → "Check me every 12 seconds"

The Mellow Mastermind approach is about being intentional with those cues. We're not aiming for minimalist perfection — we're aiming for strategic simplicity that makes the right choices obvious and the wrong choices harder.

> **DO THIS NOW: THE SPACE AUDIT REALITY CHECK**
>
> Before we redesign anything, let's get brutally honest about what you're working with.
>
> Walk through your typical creative process and answer these:
>
> 1. From deciding to create to actually starting, how many steps/obstacles are there? (Be specific: finding materials, clearing space, opening apps, etc.)
> 2. What's the first thing you see when you sit down to create? (Bills to pay? Mess to clean? Inspirational quote that now feels judgmental?)
> 3. How long does it take you to find your creative tools when inspiration strikes? (If it's more than 30 seconds, that's friction working against you)
> 4. What's your phone doing right now while you're trying to focus? (If it's within arm's reach buzzing with notifications, we have a problem)
>
> Write these answers down. This isn't self-criticism — it's intelligence gathering about what's been sabotaging your creative momentum.

The Death Zone: Your Current "Productive" Setup

Let's address the elephant in the room: that desk you call your "workspace."

It's probably covered in sticky notes with tasks from three weeks ago that you've become immune to seeing. There are abandoned journals, a candle you never light, and a plant that's barely hanging on.

You tell yourself this is your "productive zone." But if we're being real: this desk isn't where magic happens. It's where you open 23 browser tabs with good intentions, get overwhelmed by everything you "should" be doing, and then close your laptop in shame.

This desk has become the physical manifestation of your creative anxiety. It's not inspiring you — it's judging you.

We're not doing that anymore.

Build a "Play Space" Instead of a "Work Station"

Here's the revolutionary shift: Creativity = play with purpose.

Think about the last time you felt genuinely creative. I bet you weren't sitting at a sterile desk thinking "time to be productive." You were probably doodling during a meeting, having a bathroom thought, or messing around with something just for fun.

When neuroscientists study creative flow states, they find that the prefrontal cortex (your inner critic) actually quiets down. But this only happens when you feel safe to experiment. Spaces that feel formal or pressure-filled keep your inner critic on high alert. Spaces that signal "play" and "experiment" tell your brain it's safe to get weird.

The Creative Playground Design System

Here's how to transform any space — corner of bedroom, kitchen table, or dedicated studio — into creativity central:

1. The "Beautiful Failures" Station

Create a designated space for imperfect work. Label it something wonderfully, liberatingly awful:

- "Experiments in Progress"
- "Perfectly Imperfect Projects"
- "The Messy Middle Collection"
- "Zero-Stakes Creative Playground"

This is where early ideas live. Not your pristine workspace demanding perfection. A low-stakes idea vault where everything is allowed to be terrible.

Physical version: A box, drawer, or corner for sketches, voice memos, random notes; Digital version: A folder clearly labeled as experimental space

By literally naming it imperfect, you're lowering the entry barrier to zero.

2. The Ritual Station: Creativity Anchors

Motivation is like weather — unpredictable and out of your control. But rituals? Rituals are like having an umbrella. They work regardless of conditions.

Design 2-3 simple actions you can do to shift into creative mode:

For any creative:

- Light a specific candle
- Play the same 3-song playlist
- Clear one small surface and place only today's tools on it
- Write today's date at the top of a fresh page
- Change into your "creative clothes" (comfort over appearance)

The key: Consistency over complexity. Your brain needs to learn "when this happens, we create."

3. Make Starting Stupid-Easy

Most creative environments prioritize organization over access. Everything looks neat but is completely inaccessible when inspiration strikes.

The Visibility Principle: If your tools are hidden, you won't use them.

- Guitar in case → Guitar on stand
- Sketchbook in drawer → Sketchbook on desk
- Writing app buried in folders → Pinned to taskbar/dock
- Camera in bag → Camera on counter

Strategic tool placement:

- Keep one creative tool in every room that you spend time in
- Have a "grab and go" kit ready by the door

- Set up your workspace before ending each session (ready for next time)
- Keep backup supplies so you never stop creating to hunt for materials

4. The Permission Environment

Your space needs to communicate permission, not pressure. Every visual element should say "yes, try that weird thing" rather than "better make this perfect."

Visual permission cues:

- Work-in-progress displays: Show unfinished projects proudly
- Inspiration boards: Images, quotes, colors that spark joy (not productivity shame)
- Play materials: Weird pens, interesting textures, random objects that invite experimentation
- Process evidence: Keep some "beautiful mistakes" visible as reminders that imperfection leads to breakthrough

Comfort over criticism:

- Lighting that energizes, not strains
- Seating you actually want to spend time in
- Temperature you don't have to fight
- Sound that supports your thinking (silence, music, or ambient noise)

DO THIS NOW: THE 15-MINUTE SPACE SPRINT

Let's put this into practice immediately. This exercise transforms one small area into a creativity-supporting space using the Mellow Mastermind principles.

Set a timer for 15 minutes and work through these phases:

Phase 1: The Purge (Minutes 1-5)

- Clear EVERYTHING off one creative surface (desk, table, counter)
- Don't organize - just remove everything temporarily
- Put items in three quick piles: Daily use, Weekly use, Rarely/Never use
- Take a photo of your cleared space (you'll want the before/after)

Phase 2: The Strategic Return (Minutes 6-10)

- Put back ONLY items from "Daily use" pile
- Arrange them within arm's reach of where you'll sit/stand
- Everything should be accessible without getting up
- If it doesn't fit comfortably, it doesn't belong on this surface

Phase 3: The Joy Addition (Minutes 11-15)

- Add ONE thing that makes you smile (photo, plant, inspiring object)

- Add ONE thing that signals "creativity happens here" (special pen, notebook, art supply)
- Add ONE thing that removes friction (phone charger, water bottle, good lighting)
- Stand back and notice how the space feels different

Immediate Assessment: After your 15 minutes, rate the space:

- Energy level: Does this space make you want to create or avoid? (1-10)
- Friction level: How easy would it be to start working here right now? (1-10)
- Joy level: Does this space feel like YOU or like a generic office? (1-10)

If any score is below 7, spend 5 more minutes adjusting.

The Digital Environment Revolution

Your digital space is just as important as your physical one, and probably twice as chaotic.

Digital Friction vs. Digital Flow

Digital friction looks like:

- Hunting through folders for yesterday's work
- Getting distracted by notifications while trying to focus
- Forgetting which app you use for what

- Losing work because you can't remember where you saved it

Digital flow looks like:

- Project folders that make immediate sense
- Bookmarks organized by actual workflow
- Notification settings that protect focus time
- Backup systems that happen automatically

DO THIS NOW: THE 10-MINUTE DIGITAL DECLUTTER

Your digital environment creates as much friction (or flow) as your physical space.

Time needed: 10 minutes

Phase 1: Desktop Archaeology (3 minutes)

- Count files on your computer desktop: _____
- If more than 10 files, create three folders: "Current Projects," "Reference," "Archive"
- Drag files into appropriate folders
- Goal: Desktop shows only what you're actively working on

Phase 2: Browser Tab Intervention (2 minutes)

- Count open browser tabs: _____
- Close everything not related to your current creative project

- Bookmark important research in organized folders
- Start each creative session with maximum 3 relevant tabs

Phase 3: Notification Audit (3 minutes) Turn OFF notifications for:

- Social media apps (Instagram, TikTok, Twitter, Facebook)
- Non-urgent messaging (anything that isn't true emergency communication)
- News apps (creativity doesn't need constant breaking news updates)
- Shopping apps and promotional emails

Keep notifications ONLY for:

- True emergency contacts
- Calendar reminders for scheduled creative time
- Project collaboration tools you actively use

Phase 4: Creative App Access (2 minutes) Make creative tools easier to access than distracting ones:

- Pin creative apps to taskbar/dock
- Move social media apps off home screen or into buried folders
- Create desktop shortcuts for current project files
- Set creative apps to open automatically during designated creative hours

> **Results Assessment: Rate your digital environment:**
>
> - Distraction level: How easily can you access time-wasting apps? (1-10, lower is better)
> - Creative access: How quickly can you open and start your creative work? (1-10, higher is better)
> - Cognitive load: How cluttered does your digital workspace feel? (1-10, lower is better)
>
> If any score needs improvement, spend 5 more minutes making adjustments.

The Portable Creative Command Center

Not everyone has a dedicated creative space, and that's totally fine. What you need is a creative command center — everything necessary for immediate creative action in one portable container.

The Physical Kit A small bag, box, or basket containing:

- Your preferred writing tools
- Basic supplies for your medium
- Current project materials
- Small notebook or sketchpad
- Inspiration materials (photos, quotes, samples)
- Essential tech (chargers, adapters, earbuds)

The Digital Kit A folder on your desktop containing:

- Current project files
- Templates and starter documents
- Bookmark folder with research and inspiration

- Creative prompts or exercise lists
- Focus playlists

The Mental Kit A simple checklist of your creative ritual(s) so you can recreate your optimal mindset anywhere.

The Sacred Boundaries: Protecting Your Creative Space

This is where we talk about other people. Specifically, other people who see your creative time as "not real work" and your creative space as "available for other stuff."

Setting physical boundaries isn't mean — it's necessary. Your creative space needs to be protected from the invasion of daily life logistics.

DO THIS NOW: THE SACRED BOUNDARY EXPERIMENT

Time to protect your creative space from the invasion of daily life.

Time needed: 1 week (trial)

Most creative spaces get invaded by daily life logistics. This experiment helps you establish and maintain boundaries.

Choose ONE boundary to implement this week:

Option 1: The Creative Signal

- Pick a physical signal that means "creative work in progress"
- Examples: Specific hat, headphones, closed door, lit candle, sign
- Train household members: Signal = do not disturb unless emergency
- Use consistently for one week, even for 5-minute creative sessions

Option 2: The Project Sanctuary

- Designate one drawer, box, or corner as "creative materials only"
- Nothing else allowed: no bills, chores, or work documents
- Keep current project materials here
- When box/space is "open" = available for creative work
- When "closed" = creative space is off-limits to everything else

Option 3: The Time Boundary

- Choose one hour daily when your creative space serves ONLY creativity
- Examples: 7-8am, lunch hour, 8-9pm
- During this hour: no email, chores, or non-creative activities in this space
- Other family members can use space outside this hour

Option 4: The Digital Boundary

> - Create "creative time" settings on your devices
> - Phone: Do Not Disturb mode, specific apps blocked
> - Computer: Close all non-creative applications
> - Set up takes 2 minutes, saves 20+ minutes of distraction
>
> Daily Check-in Questions:
>
> 1. Did I honor my boundary today?
> 2. How did it feel to have protected creative space/time?
> 3. What tried to invade my boundary, and how did I handle it?
> 4. What adjustment would make this boundary more effective?

The Energy Zones Strategy

Not all creative work needs the same environment. Instead of one perfect workspace, create different modes within your existing space:

Thinking Mode: Comfortable seating, space to spread out notes, natural light. Where ideas percolate.

Making Mode: Easy access to tools, surfaces that can get messy, task lighting. Where ideas become real.

Refining Mode: Minimal distractions, everything organized, focus-friendly setup. Where rough becomes polished.

And The Mellow Mastermind Way To Fix It

You don't need separate rooms — you need the ability to quickly reconfigure your space based on what type of creative work you're doing.

Small Space, Big Creativity

Living in a tiny apartment or shared space? Your creative environment can still be powerful:

The Rolling Cart Solution: Everything mobile on a cart you can wheel to wherever you want to work

The Drawer Takeover: One drawer becomes your creative command center — everything you need in one place

The Wall Strategy: Vertical space for inspiration boards, tool storage, and work-in-progress displays

The Time-Share Approach: Transform the same space for different uses — dining table becomes art studio becomes writing desk

The Outdoor Office: Balcony, porch, or backyard as your creative sanctuary (weather permitting)

The Evolution Station

Your creative needs change as you grow. What supports your creativity today might constrain it in six months.

Monthly space check-ins:

- What's working well?
- What's creating friction?

- What new tools or approaches are calling to you?
- How has your creative process evolved?

Seasonal refreshes:

- Rotate inspiration materials to prevent visual habituation
- Try new organizational systems if old ones feel stale
- Experiment with different lighting or layout
- Add new elements or retire ones that no longer serve

Your environment should grow with you, not hold you back.

Remember: Your space shapes your success, but success isn't just about output. It's about sustainability, joy, and creating a practice that makes you excited to show up rather than dreading the work.

Your environment should serve you, not stress you out. Start small, stay consistent, and watch how strategic changes to your creative space can transform not just where you work, but how you think about the work itself.

The goal isn't perfection — it's removing the friction between you and your ideas. Make it easier to start than to scroll. Make it more natural to create than to consume.

Your creativity deserves a home that welcomes it with open arms.

Why You're Creatively Blocked
CHAPTER 6

The Feedback Loop
Measure Progress Without Self-Destruction

Have you ever looked at your creative work and thought, "This sucks. I suck. Maybe I should delete everything and become a barista in Portugal."

> **DO THIS NOW: THE CURRENT FEEDBACK AUDIT**
>
> Let's get honest about how you currently measure creative success:
>
> 1. What do you check first after sharing creative work? (Likes? Comments? Views? Sales? Nothing because you're too scared?)
> 2. What makes you feel like you're "succeeding" creatively? (Be specific)
> 3. What makes you feel like you're "failing"? (Also be specific)
> 4. How often do you check these metrics? (Daily? Hourly? Every time you pick up your phone?)
> 5. How do you feel after checking? (Energized? Defeated? Anxious? Neutral?)
>
> Write these down. No judgment — just data about what's been driving your creative confidence (or destroying it).

Pause. Breathe. Don't book the flight to Portugal (yet… unless you're planning a creative getaway and also planning to come back).

This chapter is about building a judgment-free feedback system — one that helps you track creative growth without spiraling into self-hate or becoming obsessed with metrics that don't actually matter.

The Problem with How We Usually Track Creative Progress

Most creators get feedback in one of two equally broken ways:

The External Validation Rollercoaster: You post something, get a rush when people respond positively, then crash when engagement drops. Your creative self-worth becomes tied to algorithmic mood swings.

The Internal Critic Torture Chamber: That voice in your head that sounds suspiciously like your middle school art teacher, cataloguing everything you did wrong and comparing your behind-the-scenes to everyone else's highlight reel.

Both systems are designed to make you feel terrible about being human.

The Third Way: Neutral Observation

What if there was another option? What if you could look at your creative work like a scientist looks at data — with curiosity instead of judgment?

This is neutral observation: noticing what's happening in your creative process without immediately slapping a "good" or "bad" label on it.

Instead of: "This painting is terrible and I'm a fraud."

Try: "I notice I'm struggling with color mixing today. Interesting."

Instead of: "Only three people liked my post. I'm obviously not cut out for this."

Try: "I'm observing that I'm feeling disappointed about the response to my work."

See the difference? One sends you into a shame spiral. The other gives you information you can actually use.

The Language Shift That Changes Everything

The words you use to describe your creative experience literally change how you experience it. Here's your new feedback vocabulary:

Old Language → New Language

- "This is garbage" → "This isn't matching my vision yet"
- "I'm not talented enough" → "I'm still developing this skill"
- "Nobody likes my work" → "This piece didn't resonate with this audience at this time"
- "I wasted my time" → "I gathered information about what doesn't work for me"
- "I'll never be good at this" → "I'm in the learning phase of this process"

This isn't toxic positivity — it's accurate assessment. You're describing what's happening instead of creating drama around what's happening.

> **DO THIS NOW: THE FEEDBACK LANGUAGE PRACTICE**
>
> For the next 3 days, catch yourself using old language about your creative work and consciously reframe it:
>
> Day 1: Just notice when you use harsh language about your work. Don't try to change it yet — just catch it happening.
>
> Day 2: When you catch harsh language, pause and reframe it using neutral observation. "I notice I'm being critical about this piece."

> Day 3: Practice the new language proactively. Before looking at your work, set the intention: "I'm going to observe what I created with curiosity."
>
> Track this in your notes app. You're training your brain to be a helpful observer instead of a cruel judge.

Building Your Personal Feedback System

Your feedback loop needs to be personal, process-focused, and actually useful for making decisions. Here's how to build one that serves you:

1. Define Success Metrics That Actually Matter

Before you can measure progress, you need to know what progress looks like FOR YOU.

Your metrics should be:

- Within your control (you can directly influence the outcome)
- Immediately measurable (you know right away if you hit them)
- Process-focused (they reward showing up and doing the work)
- Personally meaningful (they connect to why you create)

Good Metrics Examples (Specific & Measurable):

For Writers:

- ✅ "Wrote for 20 minutes without checking phone" → Track: Daily writing sessions completed

- ✅ "Finished 3 pieces this month instead of starting 10" → Track: Completion ratio

- ✅ "Shared rough draft within 24 hours of finishing" → Track: Time between completion and sharing

For Visual Artists:

- ✅ "Took progress photos without apologizing for the mess" → Track: Documentation consistency

- ✅ "Felt energized after 4 out of 5 studio sessions this week" → Track: Energy levels 1-10 post-creation

- ✅ "Learned one new technique through experimentation" → Track: Skills attempted/practiced

For Musicians:

- ✅ "Had genuine conversation about my music with someone new" → Track: Meaningful music discussions

- ✅ "Recorded voice memos of 3 melody ideas during commute" → Track: Idea capture frequency

✅ "Finished song sketches instead of perfecting first 30 seconds" → Track: Complete song demos

Terrible Metrics Examples (External & Uncontrollable):

What NOT to Track:

❌ "Getting 100+ likes on Instagram posts" → You can't control the algorithm

❌ "Making $5,000 this month from creative work" → Too many external factors

❌ "Being featured in [specific publication]" → Not your decision to make

❌ "Having work that looks like [famous creator]'s work" → Comparison-based, not growth-based

Notice how the good metrics are about your behavior and internal experience? That's intentional.

2. Track Leading Indicators, Not Just Outcomes

Most people obsess over lagging indicators — end results that are largely out of their control. Leading indicators are the actions that influence those outcomes. The things you have direct control over:

Input Indicators (What you put in):

- Days you showed up to create
- Time spent creating vs. consuming
- New techniques you experimented with

- Creative risks you took
- Ideas you captured instead of letting slip away

Process Indicators (How you work):

- Average time to start creating (friction measurement)
- Percentage of sessions where you reached flow state
- Consistency of creative practice
- Quality of your creative environment
- How often you push through initial resistance

Output Indicators (What you produce):

- Projects completed (regardless of "quality")
- Experiments tried
- Pieces shared publicly
- Skills developed
- Creative problems solved

Impact Indicators (How it affects you and others):

- Personal satisfaction with work
- Growth in technical abilities
- Meaningful conversations sparked
- Positive feedback received
- Alignment with your creative values

The magic ratio: Focus 70% of your attention on input and process indicators, 30% on output and impact indicators.

How to Measure "Feeling Energized" Practically

Energy Assessment Scale (Rate 1-10 after each creative session):

- 1-3: Drained, need recovery time, regret starting
- 4-6: Neutral, neither energized nor depleted
- 7-10: Energized, excited about next session, feel accomplished

Track patterns: What conditions lead to 7+ energy ratings?

Example Energy Tracking:

- Monday, 9am writing, coffee shop → Energy: 8/10
- Tuesday, 3pm painting, home studio → Energy: 4/10
- Wednesday, 7pm music, bedroom setup → Energy: 9/10

Pattern discovered: Morning writing sessions and evening music creation = highest energy

What Constitutes a "Genuine Conversation" About Work

Genuine Creative Conversation Checklist:

- Someone asked follow-up questions about your process
- You explained a creative challenge you're working through
- They shared their own creative struggles or insights
- The conversation lasted longer than 2 minutes
- You felt understood rather than judged
- You learned something or gained new perspective

Examples:

- ✅ "How do you decide when a poem is finished?" followed by 10-minute discussion

- ✅ Explaining your song's inspiration and having someone relate it to their experience

- ❌ "Cool" response to sharing your work with no follow-up

- ❌ Generic compliments without engagement ("Nice!")

> **DO THIS NOW: DESIGN YOUR PERSONAL DASHBOARD**
>
> Create a simple tracking system that you'll actually use:
>
> 1. Pick 3-5 metrics from the categories above that genuinely matter to you
> 2. Choose your tracking method:
>   - Simple notes app on your phone
>   - One-page monthly calendar
>   - Basic spreadsheet
>   - Physical notebook
>   - Voice memos to yourself
> 3. Set a weekly check-in time (5 minutes max) to review your metrics
> 4. Focus on trends, not daily fluctuations — you're looking for patterns over time
>
> Example dashboard:
>
> - Days I showed up: ✓✓✗✓✓✗✓ (5/7 this week)

- Average start time: 8 minutes (down from 15 last week!)
- Projects completed: 1 (finished that poem I've been working on)
- Energy after creating: Mostly good (4/5 sessions felt energizing)
- New things tried: Experimented with watercolors

The Weekly Creative Check-In System

Every week, have a friendly conversation with yourself. Not a performance review — a curious check-in about what you're learning about yourself from your data gathering.

The Four Questions:

1. What worked well this week? (Not what was perfect, just what worked)
2. What felt sticky or difficult? (Not what was terrible, just what didn't flow)
3. What did I learn? (About your process, preferences, or craft)
4. What wants to be explored next? (Stay curious, not prescriptive)

Example check-in: *What worked:* "Had three solid creative sessions. Working right after tea before checking email really helped. The new playlist put me in a good headspace."

What felt sticky: "Tried working at the kitchen table twice and got distracted by dishes. Also, that one project feels stuck — not sure what direction to take it."

What I learned: "I'm definitely more focused in the morning. I also work better when my environment is clean and designated for creating."

What wants exploring: "Curious about trying a different approach to that stuck project. Also want to experiment with working outside — saw someone doing that and it looked peaceful."

DO THIS NOW: YOUR FIRST WEEKLY CHECK-IN

Set a recurring reminder for the same time every week (Sunday evening or Monday morning work well). Spend exactly 10 minutes answering the four questions.

Do this in whatever format feels natural — voice memo, typed notes, handwritten journal, or even talking to a friend. The key is consistency and honest observation without judgment.

Quick Weekly Review Template Save this to your phone's notes app:

This week's creative wins: _____

This week's sticky points: _____

Next week's one focus: _____

Energy check (1-10): _____

The Progress Portfolio: Evidence of Growth

Create a simple record of your creative journey that you can look back on when you're feeling stuck or discouraged.

Digital options:

- Monthly photo collages of everything you created
- Screenshot collection of positive feedback or breakthrough moments
- Simple folder of work samples from different time periods
- Audio journal entries about creative insights
- Private Instagram account documenting your process

Physical options:

- Photo album of work in progress and finished pieces
- Journal dedicated to creative insights and growth observations
- Wall display showing evolution over time
- Box of physical samples from different phases

The key: Make it yours and keep it private. This isn't for anyone else — it's evidence for you that growth is happening, even when it doesn't feel like it.

The "Delete Count" Revolution

Here's a radical idea: track what you're willing to throw away.

Most creators measure success by output: words written, songs finished, pieces posted. But what if we measured by what you were willing to delete?

- That sketch you scrapped after version 3?
- That poem that led to a better one?
- That melody you recorded six times before nailing it?
- That business idea you tested and pivoted from?

That's all progress. You were in the game. Deleting is part of creating.

Professional creatives have hard drives full of "failed" experiments. They're not failures — they're the cost of finding the good stuff. Your willingness to delete is a sign of developing taste and creative courage.

> **DO THIS NOW: START A "BEAUTIFUL FAILURES" COLLECTION**
>
> Instead of deleting abandoned projects, create a folder (digital or physical) and name it something like:
>
> - "Experiments That Taught Me Something"
> - "Creative Compost"
> - "The Learning Archive"
> - "Attempts That Mattered"
>
> What goes in here:
>
> - Rough drafts you scrapped for better versions
> - Projects you started but pivoted away from
> - "Failed" experiments that led to breakthroughs

- Work that didn't resonate but taught you something

Monthly Review Questions:

1. What patterns do I see in my "failures"?
2. What did each experiment teach me about my process?
3. Are there any "failed" ideas worth revisiting with a new perspective?
4. How has my taste/skill evolved since creating these?

This archive becomes evidence of your creative growth and willingness to experiment - both crucial for long-term creative development.

The Experimental Mindset

Smart creators don't guess what will work — they test constantly. They treat everything as a low-stakes experiment.

- Start small and cheap — low stakes make feedback easier to handle
- Test one variable at a time — so you know what actually worked
- Separate your identity from each experiment — you're testing ideas, not yourself
- Use feedback to inform next experiments — data, not validation

For Writers:

- Share excerpts before writing full pieces
- Test different headlines for the same content
- Try various opening paragraphs with different audiences
- Experiment with different formats (threads, newsletters, stories)

For Visual Artists:

- Post process shots, not just finished pieces
- Share color palette tests or composition experiments
- Get feedback on sketches before investing in final versions
- Try the same subject in different styles

For Musicians:

- Share 30-second clips of melody ideas
- Test different arrangements with small audiences
- Try the same song in different genres or moods
- Record voice memos of rough ideas

DO THIS NOW: DESIGN YOUR FIRST CREATIVE EXPERIMENT

Pick something you've been wanting to try but haven't because it feels too risky:

1. Make it smaller — what's the tiniest version you could test?

> 2. Make it cheaper — how could you test this with minimal time/resource investment?
> 3. Make it faster — how quickly could you get feedback on this idea?
> 4. Make it specific — what exactly are you testing, and how will you measure the result?
>
> Example: Instead of "write a book about productivity," try "write a 500-word post about one productivity technique and see if it helps anyone."
>
> Launch your experiment this week. Focus on learning, not succeeding.

Handling Feedback Without Losing Your Mind

Eventually, you'll get external feedback on your work. Some will be helpful, some will be weird, some will be mean. Here's how to process it without spiraling:

The Feedback Filtering System

Before reading feedback, ask:

1. Is this person my intended audience? (If not, their opinion matters less)
2. Are they offering specific, actionable input? (Vague praise or criticism isn't useful)
3. Do they have relevant experience or expertise? (Context matters)
4. Are they commenting on the work or attacking me personally? (Only engage with work-focused feedback)

The 24-Hour Rule

When you receive strong feedback (positive or negative), wait 24 hours before making any major decisions about your work or creative direction.

The "So What?" Technique

When criticism stings, try this progression: "They said my work is [whatever]." So what? "People might think I'm not good at this." So what? "Maybe I should quit." So what? "I'd never get to experience the joy of creating again."

Usually by the third "so what?" you realize the thing you're catastrophizing about isn't actually catastrophic.

Long-Term Sustainability: The Decades Game

The most important feedback loop isn't between you and your audience — it's between you and your future self. Every time you complete your feedback cycle (create → track → reflect → adjust), you're building evidence that you can learn and improve.

This creates what psychologists call "creative self-efficacy" — the belief that you can successfully create meaningful work. This is way more valuable than external validation because it's yours and nobody can take it away.

Signs you're building creative self-efficacy:

- You're more excited about the process than the outcome
- Setbacks feel like data instead of personal failures

Why You're Creatively Blocked

- You trust your own creative instincts more
- You're less dependent on external validation
- You bounce back faster from disappointments
- You take more creative risks because you know you can handle whatever happens

Remember: The goal isn't to optimize every aspect of your creative process. The goal is to build a sustainable relationship with your creativity that honors both your ambition and your humanity.

Your feedback loop should motivate you, not torment you. If tracking becomes another source of pressure or self-criticism, it's time to step back and remember why you started creating in the first place.

The numbers are just information. Your worth as a human isn't on the spreadsheet.

Keep creating. Keep observing. Keep being kind to yourself in the process.

And The Mellow Mastermind Way To Fix It

Why You're Creatively Blocked
CHAPTER 7

When to Ignore All This Advice

Sometimes the Most Creative Thing You Can Do... Is Stop

Here's a confession that might break your brain: Everything you've read in this book? The strategies, the systems, the clever frameworks and life-changing mindset shifts?

Sometimes, you need to ignore all of it.

> **DO THIS NOW: THE BLOCK VS. BURNOUT DIAGNOSTIC**
>
> Before we go any further, let's figure out what you're dealing with. Read both lists and notice which one makes you go "oh snap, that's me!":
>
> Creative Block feels like:
>
> - Frustration with a specific project or challenge
> - Having creative energy but can't access it
> - Wanting to create but feeling stuck or confused
> - Procrastination that feels like avoidance
> - Comparing your work to others and feeling inadequate
> - Perfectionism preventing you from starting

- A specific fear or resistance you can name

Creative Burnout feels like:

- Exhaustion that sleep doesn't fix
- Feeling disconnected from work you used to love
- Everything creative feels like another chore on your endless to-do list
- No energy for ANY creative work, not just your main project
- Resentment toward your creative practice
- Physical symptoms: headaches, tension, fatigue
- Going through the motions without feeling present
- Loss of curiosity about things that used to excite you
- Dreading creative time instead of looking forward to it

If you're blocked: Use the tools in this book. Push through gently. Experiment with different approaches.

If you're burnt out: Close the book. Rest. Come back when your nervous system has recovered.

I'm serious about that second part.

This Is the Plot Twist Nobody Talks About

We're so obsessed with productivity hacks and creative breakthroughs that we've forgotten something crucial: Your creative system is only as sustainable as the human operating it.

Here's the thing about humans that the productivity industrial complex doesn't want you to remember: We're not machines. We have seasons. We have cycles. We have days when our creative well runs dry not because we're blocked, but because we've been drawing from it without ever filling it back up. Sometimes even the gentlest productivity advice becomes pressure. If you find yourself:

- Forcing 5-minute sessions when you need 5-hour naps (Chapter 4 misapplied)
- Perfectionist about shipping at 70% (Chapter 3 irony)
- Obsessively tracking rest metrics (Chapter 6 gone wrong)
- Feeling guilty about your creative environment (Chapter 5 pressure)

...then it's time to step back from ALL systems and remember: you are more than your creative output.

The Burnout Trap: When Productivity Becomes Poison

Here's where it gets tricky. When you're burnt out, your brain often tries to solve it with MORE productivity strategies. "Maybe if I just find the right system, the right schedule, the right hack..."

But trying to productive-hack your way out of burnout is like trying to sprint your way out of quicksand. The harder you struggle, the deeper you sink.

> *Burnout isn't a productivity problem — it's a sustainability problem.*

And sustainability isn't about finding the perfect system. It's about honoring your human limitations and working WITH them instead of constantly trying to transcend them.

> **DO THIS NOW: THE BURNOUT REALITY CHECK**
>
> If you identified with the burnout list above, let's get honest about what it's costing you:
>
> 1. How long have you been feeling this way? (Weeks? Months? "I can't remember feeling excited about creating"?)
> 2. What are you trying to push through? (Specific projects, general creative output, social media presence?)
> 3. What's driving the pressure to keep going? (Money? Deadlines? Fear of losing momentum? Other people's expectations?)
> 4. What would happen if you stopped for a week? (Write down the actual consequences, not your anxiety's horror movie)
> 5. What would feel genuinely restorative right now? (Not "productive rest" like reading about creativity — actual rest)
>
> Keep these answers nearby. We're going to need them.

The Permission Slip You Didn't Know You Needed

Ready for this? You have permission to stop.

You have permission to take a break without having a "good enough" reason. You have permission to rest without earning it first. You have permission to say no to creative opportunities that don't serve you right now.

You have permission to be a human being instead of a creative content machine.

This isn't giving up. This isn't lazy. This isn't failure. This is strategic sustainability — the kind that lets you create for decades instead of burning out spectacularly in a few years.

The Art of Creative Fallow Periods

Farmers know something we've forgotten: soil needs to rest between growing seasons. If you plant crop after crop without letting the land recover, eventually nothing will grow no matter how much you water it or how perfect your technique.

Your creative consciousness works the same way. It needs fallow periods — times when you're not actively producing, but you're not inactive either.

During creative fallow periods, you're:

- Consuming instead of creating — Reading books, watching films, going to museums, listening to music
- Living instead of documenting — Having experiences without immediately turning them into content
- Playing instead of producing — Engaging with creativity for joy, not output
- Reflecting instead of reacting — Processing what you've learned and created so far
- Resting instead of rushing — Letting your nervous system reset

What fallow periods look like in practice:

- Taking a week off from your main creative project
- Switching to a completely different creative medium temporarily
- Engaging with creativity as a consumer rather than creator
- Spending time in nature without your phone
- Having conversations about ideas without pressure to act on them
- Letting yourself be bored (seriously, when's the last time you were actually bored?)
- Doing creative activities with no intention of sharing or improving

Design Your Fallow Period

If you're burnt out, you need to actively plan rest the same way you'd plan a project:

1. Choose your timeframe: Start small — even 3 days can help. Work up to a week or more if needed.
2. Set boundaries: What will you NOT do during this time? (Check work email? Post on social media? Think about your creative projects?)
3. Fill the void: What will you do instead? (Read fiction? Take walks? Cook elaborate meals? Sleep 10 hours a night?)
4. Communicate: Who needs to know you're taking a break? What do you need to say to manage expectations?
5. Plan your return: How will you ease back into creating? (Spoiler: not by immediately trying to catch up on everything)

Important: This isn't a "productive break" where you optimize your rest or learn new skills. This is genuine, no-agenda restoration time.

The Seasons of Creative Life

Your creative energy isn't linear — it's cyclical. Just like natural seasons, each phase serves a purpose, and you can't skip or rush through them:

Creative Spring (The Planting Season):

- High energy and enthusiasm
- Lots of new ideas and project starts
- Excitement about possibilities
- Natural time for beginning things

Creative Summer (The Growing Season):

- Sustained focus and productivity
- Making steady progress on projects
- Building skills and momentum
- Natural time for deep work and completion

Creative Fall (The Harvest Season):

- Completing and sharing finished work
- Reflecting on what you've learned
- Preparing for the next phase
- Natural time for editing, refining, publishing

Creative Winter (The Rest Season):

- Lower energy and motivation
- Time for reflection and planning
- Consuming rather than creating
- Natural time for rest and renewal

> **The key insight:** *You can't force spring, you can't skip winter, and you can't harvest all year round.*

Most burnt-out creators are trying to live in permanent summer, wondering why they're exhausted.

DO THIS NOW: IDENTIFY YOUR CURRENT SEASON

Look at your creative life right now:

1. What season does your energy feel like? (High and excited? Focused and productive? Ready to share and complete? Tired and need rest?)
2. What season are you trying to force yourself into? (Are you trying to plant new seeds when you need to harvest? Trying to produce when you need to rest?)
3. What would honoring your actual season look like? (What activities, pace, and focus would align with where you actually are?)
4. What's one thing you can do this week to better align with your natural creative season?

Stop fighting your seasons. Work with them.

Why You're Creatively Blocked

When Your Tools Stop Working (The Warning Signs)

You know you're in burnout territory when your usual creative strategies start feeling like punishment instead of support:

- Your 5-minute timer feels like a prison sentence
- Your morning pages feel like homework
- Your productivity system makes you want to throw your laptop out the window
- Your creative space feels like a guilt shrine
- Other people's creative success makes you feel bitter instead of inspired
- You're creating content about being creative instead of just being creative

This is your cue to put down all the tools. Not forever. Not permanently. Just for now.

The Tool Addiction Warning Signs:

- You feel guilty when you're not implementing productivity strategies
- You judge your creative worth by how well you follow systems
- You spend more time optimizing than creating
- You feel like a failure when systems don't work for you
- You panic at the thought of creating without a system

When systems become identity instead of support, it's time to step back.

Case Study: Agatha Christie's Career-Saving Sabbatical

In 1926, Agatha Christie seemed to have it all. Successful mystery writer, beloved characters, growing audience. But behind the scenes, her life was falling apart: her mother died, her husband asked for a divorce, and she was emotionally and creatively exhausted.

So, in 1928, she made a radical decision: she stopped writing novels entirely for nearly two years.

What she did during her sabbatical:

- Traveled to archaeological sites in the Middle East
- Got completely away from the writing world
- Focused on rebuilding her personal life
- Gave her mind permission to NOT think about writing

What she didn't do:

- Write "just a little bit" to stay in practice
- Study her craft or read mystery novels
- Plan her comeback or worry about her career
- Feel guilty about the break

The result: When Christie returned to writing in 1930, she introduced Miss Jane Marple and entered what many consider her most creative and successful period.

> **The math:** *Two years of rest enabled forty years of sustainable creativity. That's a 20:1 return on investment.*

> ## DO THIS NOW: THE "WHAT WOULD ACTUALLY HAPPEN?" EXERCISE
>
> Your brain is probably screaming about all the terrible things that will happen if you take a break. Let's reality-check those fears:
>
> 1. Write down your biggest fear about taking creative time off (losing momentum? People forgetting about you? Missing opportunities?)
> 2. What's the actual, realistic worst-case scenario? (Not your anxiety's disaster movie — the real worst case)
> 3. What's the best-case scenario of taking rest when you need it? (Coming back refreshed? Having better ideas? Creating more sustainable work?)
> 4. What's the worst-case scenario of NOT taking a break? (Complete burnout? Hating your work? Quitting entirely?)
> 5. Who do you know who took a creative break and was fine? (Or better than fine?)
>
> Usually, the fear of stopping is way worse than the actual consequences of strategic rest.

The Creative Detox Protocol

When you recognize you're burnt out, here's your step-by-step recovery plan:

And The Mellow Mastermind Way To Fix It

Phase 1: Stop Defending Your Tiredness (Week 1)

You don't need to justify why you're exhausted. You don't need to prove you've "earned" rest. Burnout isn't a character flaw — it's information from your system.

This week:

- Give yourself permission to feel tired without shame
- Stop comparing your capacity to others'
- Notice how much energy you spend justifying your need for rest
- Practice saying "I'm taking a break" without explanation

Phase 2: Rest Without Improvement (Week 2-3)

This is the hardest part for recovering productivity addicts: rest that doesn't come with homework.

What this looks like:

- Take naps without setting alarms
- Watch TV without feeling guilty
- Sit in silence without meditating "properly"
- Go for walks without podcasts
- Do things that serve no purpose except they feel good

What to avoid:

- "Productive rest" like learning new skills
- Planning your creative comeback
- Reading about creativity or productivity

Why You're Creatively Blocked

- Organizing your creative materials
- Any activity with a measurable outcome

Phase 3: Let Things Be Undone (Ongoing)

The emails can wait. The project can pause. Your social media can go quiet. The world will continue spinning without your constant creative input.

Phase 4: Remember That Fallow Is Fertile (Week 4+)

Fields that lay fallow aren't lazy — they're gathering nutrients for next season's growth. Your creative sabbatical is doing the same thing, even when it doesn't feel like it.

Trust that:

- Ideas are still percolating below conscious awareness
- Your creative muscles aren't disappearing from disuse
- Rest is active preparation for future work
- You're not falling behind — you're investing in sustainability

---

DO THIS NOW: CREATE YOUR BACK-TO-WORK PROTOCOL

Before you take your break, plan how you'll return to creating (this reduces anxiety about the rest period):

1. Set a tentative return date — but give yourself permission to extend if needed

2. Plan a gentle re-entry — don't try to immediately return to full capacity
3. Start with your smallest, easiest creative act — maybe just 5 minutes of the thing you used to love
4. Lower your standards — your first work back doesn't need to compensate for the time off
5. Check in with your energy — if you still feel burnt out, extend the break

Remember: The goal isn't to return exactly where you left off. It's to return with renewed energy and perspective.

The Counter-Intuitive Truth

The most creative thing you can do when you're burnt out isn't finding a better system, a more inspiring workspace, or a more motivating deadline.

The most creative thing you can do is trust the process of not creating.

This isn't about waiting for inspiration to strike. It's about respecting the natural rhythms of creative life. It's about understanding that creativity isn't just about output — it's about the full cycle of inspiration, creation, completion, and renewal.

Early Warning Signs (Catch Burnout Before It Catches You)

You don't have to wait until you're completely fried. Here are the early signals that it's time to pause:

- Your creative work feels like obligation more often than invitation
- You're more worried about maintaining streaks than enjoying the process
- You find yourself creating content ABOUT being creative instead of just creating
- You're constantly seeking external validation for your creative choices
- You feel guilty when you're not creating
- You've lost touch with WHY you started creating in the first place

The early intervention: Take a weekend off. Not a working weekend or a "productive" weekend — a genuine break from creative output. See how it feels.

The "But I Can't Afford to Stop" Reality Check

I hear you. Rent is due. Client deadlines loom. The algorithm demands consistent content. You feel like you can't afford to take a break.

But here's what I learned the hard way: You can't afford NOT to take a break.

Burnt-out work is low-quality work. Burnt-out creators make poor decisions. Burnt-out humans get sick, make mistakes, and eventually crash anyway — but without the strategic planning.

Strategic approaches:

- Plan breaks between projects instead of in the middle of them
- Communicate proactively with clients about your need for sustainable pacing
- Build rest into your pricing — charge enough that you can afford to take breaks
- Create systems that work without constant input — batch content, automate what you can
- Start small — even 3 days can make a significant difference

The Plot Twist: Rest Is Rebellious

In a culture that glorifies the grind, rest is a radical act. In a world that measures worth by output, choosing to pause is revolutionary.

Your creative practice doesn't have to be a relentless march toward some imaginary finish line. It can be a dance — sometimes fast, sometimes slow, sometimes perfectly still.

The goal isn't to create more. The goal is to create sustainably. And sustainability requires the wisdom to know when to push forward and when to rest.

Do This Now: Write Yourself a Permission Letter

Take 5 minutes and write yourself a letter from your future creative self — the one who learned to rest without guilt:

Start with: "Dear [your name], I'm writing to tell you something you need to hear..."

Include:

- Permission to rest when you need it
- Reassurance that the work will be there when you return
- Recognition of your humanity beyond your creative output
- Wisdom about the seasons of creative life
- Love for who you are, not just what you make

Keep this letter where you can find it when burnout strikes. You'll need the reminder that rest isn't failure — it's strategy.

And The Mellow Mastermind Way To Fix It

A Love Letter to Your Future Creative Self

Dear Creator,

The work will be there when you get back. The ideas will be there when you're ready. The world will not end if you take a break.

In fact, the world might be better for it. Because a well-rested, inspired creator makes work that resonates deeper than anything produced from depletion.

So, close the laptop. Put down the pen. Step away from the easel. Turn off the notifications.

Your creative practice loves you enough to wait.

And when you're ready — when you're really, really ready, not just guilty-ready — it will welcome you back with open arms and fresh possibilities.

Sometimes the most creative thing you can do is remember that you are infinitely more than what you make.

Rest well, Your Future Creative Self

Why You're Creatively Blocked

Your creativity will wait. It always does.

The most productive thing you can do right now might be absolutely nothing. And that's not just okay — it's exactly what your creative life needs.

Trust the process. Rest when you need to. Create when you're called to.

Your future work will thank you for learning the difference.

And The Mellow Mastermind Way To Fix It

Why You're Creatively Blocked

CHAPTER 8

The Mellow Mastermind Lifestyle

How to Stay Unblocked Without Losing Your Chill

Congrats! You now have more creative strategies than a productivity guru's Pinterest board! You've learned to start before you're ready, ship at 70%, remix like a pro, design environments that support flow, build feedback loops that don't destroy your soul, and even recognize when to ignore all advice and rest instead.

But now what?

This is where most creativity books abandon you — with a toolkit but no operating manual. They give you tactics without philosophy, quick fixes without sustainable systems, strategies without the wisdom to know when and how to combine them.

> **DO THIS NOW: THE CREATIVE INTEGRATION AUDIT**
>
> Before we build your lifestyle, let's assess what you're actually working with:

> Time needed: 5 minutes
>
> 1. Which chapter's main technique have you actually tried? (Be honest — reading about it doesn't count)
> 2. What's your biggest creative challenge right now? (Specific situation, not general "I'm blocked")
> 3. When you imagine your ideal creative practice, what does a typical Tuesday look like? (Not Saturday — Tuesday, when life is life-ing)
> 4. What's one creative habit you've maintained for more than a month? (This shows what actually sticks, according to your personality)
> 5. Rate your current creative energy: Depleted (1-3), Okay (4-6), or Energized (7-10)
>
> Keep these answers visible — they're the foundation for everything we're about to build.

The Real Victory Isn't Perfection

Here's what I wish someone had told me when I was drowning in productivity content and creative anxiety: The goal isn't to become some zen master of creativity who never struggles, never procrastinates, and always knows exactly what to create next.

The goal is to become someone who can work with their human messiness instead of constantly fighting against it.

You're going to have days when you ignore every single thing in this book and fall back into old patterns. You're going to procrastinate on social media for three hours, then shame-spiral about it. You're going to start seventeen different projects and finish none of them.

And you know what? That's not failure. That's just being human on a week day.

The Mellow Mastermind lifestyle is not about never struggling — it's about struggling more skillfully, with better tools, and waayyy less dramatic inner monologue.

Your New Default Settings

Instead of trying to optimize every aspect of your creative practice, focus on shifting your default responses. When you're not actively thinking about it, what do you automatically do?

Old Defaults:

- When stuck → push harder
- When tired → caffeinate and force it
- When blocked → try to break through with willpower
- When scared → avoid and procrastinate
- When imperfect → hide until it's better

New Defaults:

- When stuck → get curious about the resistance
- When tired → rest without guilt or timeline
- When blocked → start smaller and simpler
- When scared → start anyway for just five minutes
- When imperfect → share it and gather real feedback

These defaults become your creative operating system — the responses that kick in when you're not actively managing your process.

The Three Pillars of Mellow Mastermind Living

After working with hundreds of creative humans, I've noticed that the ones who stay unblocked long-term all share three core practices:

Pillar 1: Permission-Based Creating

This is the foundation of everything. Before each creative session, spend 30 seconds asking:

1. What would feel most alive to work on right now?
2. What permission do I need to give myself today?
3. What would I create if no one else would ever see it?
4. What would be fun to explore, even if it leads nowhere?

Maybe you need permission to:

- Make something just for you (not for your audience)
- Work on the "wrong" project (the one that excites you)
- Take a creative detour (following curiosity instead of your plan)
- Change your mind mid-project (pivoting isn't failure)
- Create something that doesn't fit your "brand"
- Experiment with a new medium or style
- Make something that serves no purpose except joy
- Stop working on something that isn't serving you

Pillar 2: Rhythm-Based Working

You're not a machine, and machines don't have natural rhythms. But humans do. Your job as a Mellow Mastermind is to discover your rhythms and work with them instead of against them.

Keep a simple note on your phone for two weeks. After each creative session, jot down:

- Time of day
- Energy level (1-10)
- Environment where you worked
- What felt easy vs. sticky
- Overall satisfaction with the session

Don't try to optimize as you go — just gather data. Patterns will emerge naturally.

Common Creative Rhythms:

- The Morning Glory: Peak creativity happens before 10 AM
- The Night Owl: Creative energy peaks after 8 PM
- The Sprint Worker: Intense 90-minute sessions followed by complete breaks
- The Background Processor: Needs time between sessions for ideas to percolate
- The Seasonal Creator: Energy fluctuates with actual seasons or life phases
- The Steady Eddie: Prefers consistent, moderate daily practice

There's no right rhythm — only your rhythm.

Pillar 3: Joy-Based Decisions

When deciding what to create, how to spend your creative time, or which projects to pursue, you factor in joy alongside practical considerations.

Not joy as in "everything must be fun all the time," but joy as in "does this connect me to why I started creating in the first place?"

The Joy Audit (Monthly Practice):

Once a month, look at your creative commitments and ask:

- Which projects make me excited to sit down and work?
- Which feel like obligation or drudgery?
- Where am I creating from? Fear or curiosity?
- What would I work on if I knew it would succeed?
- What would I work on if I knew it would fail but be fun?

This isn't about only working on "fun" projects. It's about understanding which projects connect you to your creative why and which are just busy work disguised as creativity.

The Mellow Mastermind Toolkit: When to Use What

You now have multiple techniques from different chapters. Here's your decision tree for which tool to reach for when:

Why You're Creatively Blocked

> 📋 **Quick Reference: The Creative Emergency Toolkit (When to Use What)**
>
> **When you can't start:**
>
> - **First try:** 5-Minute Trick (Chapter 4)
> - **If that fails:** Change environment (Chapter 5)
> - **Still stuck:** Check if you need permission (Pillar 1) or rest (Chapter 7)
>
> **When everything feels overwhelming:**
>
> - **First try:** Brain dump + choose one tiny thing
> - **Support with:** Environment clearing (Chapter 5)
> - **Remember:** 70% Rule (Chapter 3) — you don't need to do everything perfectly
>
> **When perfectionism strikes:**
>
> - **First try:** Set today's deadline + 70% shipping (Chapter 3)
> - **Support with:** Deliberately create something terrible first
> - **Remember:** Progress tracking (Chapter 6) focuses on completion, not perfection
>
> **When you keep getting distracted:**

- **First try:** Environment modification — phone away, distractions removed (Chapter 5)
- **Support with:** 5-minute focus sessions (Chapter 4)
- **Check:** Are you distracted or actually tired? Different solutions needed.

When you feel lost or directionless:

- **First try:** Return to your influences — what excited you originally? (Chapter 2)
- **Support with:** Joy audit — what actually energizes you?
- **Consider:** Might be time for a fallow period (Chapter 7)

Daily Rhythms of a Mellow Mastermind

Morning Routine (Flexible, Not Rigid)

Energy Check (30 seconds): How are you feeling today? No judgment, just data.

Permission Setting (30 seconds): What do you need permission to do today?

Tiny Commitment (1 minute): What's the smallest creative thing you could do that would feel like a win?

Why You're Creatively Blocked

This isn't about becoming a morning person if you're not one. It's about starting each day with intentional connection to your creative self, whenever your day actually begins.

During Creative Work

- Start with your established rhythm: Use what you learned about your natural patterns.
- Apply your tools based on current need: Don't use every technique every time. Match the tool to the current challenge.
- Honor your energy: If you're at 3/10 energy, don't expect 8/10 output. Adjust expectations and approach accordingly.
- Practice neutral observation: Notice what's happening without immediately judging it as good or bad.

End of Day Reflection (2 minutes max)

- Celebrate showing up: Did you honor your creative commitment? Even five minutes counts.
- Note what worked: What conditions, timing, or approach supported your creativity today?
- Set up tomorrow: Leave breadcrumbs for your future self (remember Hemingway's mid-sentence technique).
- Release the outcome: You did your part; the results aren't entirely up to you.

> **Practice This Week: Design Your Personal Daily Rhythm**
>
> Based on what you learned about your patterns, create a simple daily structure:
>
> My optimal creative time: _____
>
> My creative energy prep: _____
>
> My minimum viable creative action:
> _____
>
> My end-of-session ritual: _____
>
> Try this structure for one week, then adjust based on what actually happens (not what you think should happen).

Common Mellow Mastermind Challenges (And How to Handle Them)

Even with all these tools and mindsets, you'll face specific challenges as you build this lifestyle. Here are the most common ones:

Challenge 1: "This Feels Too Easy"

You've been conditioned to believe that if creative work isn't difficult, painful, or stressful, you're not doing it right. The Mellow Mastermind approach can feel suspiciously simple.

The Reframe: Easy doesn't mean effortless. It means sustainable. You're not cheating by working with your natural tendencies instead of against them.

Challenge 2: "Everyone Else Is Doing More"

Social media makes it look like everyone else is more productive, inspired, and successful. Your 5-minute daily sessions feel pathetic compared to someone's 8-hour creative marathons.

The Reframe: You're seeing their highlight reel, not their behind-the-scenes. Your consistent small actions compound over time in ways that dramatic unsustainable efforts don't.

Challenge 3: "I'm Not Making Enough Progress"

Progress in creative work is often invisible until it suddenly becomes visible. You might not see growth day-to-day, but over months and years, the compound effect is dramatic.

The Reframe: Track process metrics, not just outcome metrics. Showing up consistently IS progress, even when individual sessions feel unproductive.

Challenge 4: "What If I'm Being Too Soft on Myself?"

There's a difference between being compassionate and being indulgent. You might worry that the Mellow Mastermind approach lacks the discipline needed for real achievement.

The Reframe: Self-compassion is strategic. It helps you bounce back from setbacks faster, take more creative risks, and maintain motivation over the long term.

Challenge 5: "I Miss the Drama"

Some creators are addicted to the emotional intensity of deadline pressure, creative crises, and last-minute inspiration. The Mellow Mastermind approach can feel boring by comparison.

The Reframe: Drama is expensive. It might feel exciting, but it's not sustainable. Channel that energy into your work, not your work process.

Building Your Creative Community

The Mellow Mastermind lifestyle isn't meant to be lived in isolation. You need people who understand that rest days are as important as productive days, who celebrate small wins, and who support sustainable creativity over hustle culture.

Community Building Strategies:

- Find your creative peers: People working on similar challenges, not necessarily the same medium. The writer and the musician might have more in common than two writers at different stages.
- Seek supportive accountability: People who check in on your wellbeing, not just your output. "How are you feeling about your creative practice?" vs. "How much did you produce this week?"
- Share your process, not just your products: Let people see the messy middle, the experiments, the failures. This gives them permission to be human too.
- Celebrate others without comparison: Practice genuinely celebrating others' success without making it about your own perceived lack.

Long-Term Sustainability: The Decades Game

The Mellow Mastermind lifestyle isn't about maximizing creative output this year. It's about building a relationship with creativity that can last decades.

The 10-Year Vision Exercise:

Imagine yourself in 10 years, still creating consistently and joyfully. Answer these questions:

1. What kind of creator do you want to be known as? (Process-focused, not achievement-focused)
2. What themes or questions do you want to explore? (The through-lines of your work)
3. How do you want to feel about your creative practice? (The internal experience you're building toward)
4. What legacy do you want your creative work to have? (Impact, not just output)

Work backward from this vision: What daily practices, boundaries, and choices would support this long-term creative identity?

The Integration Challenge: Your Next 30 Days

Here's your blueprint for integrating everything you've learned into a sustainable creative lifestyle:

Week 1: Foundation Setting

- Choose your primary block type and one main technique to focus on

- Establish your minimum viable creative practice (5 minutes daily minimum)
- Begin rhythm tracking (energy, timing, environment)

Week 2: Environment Optimization

- Do the 15-minute space sprint from Chapter 5
- Implement one digital boundary (phone settings, app organization, etc.)
- Notice how environment changes affect your creative sessions

Week 3: System Integration

- Add one secondary technique from another chapter
- Practice combining tools (5-minute start + environment setup + 70% shipping)
- Do your first weekly review using the questions from this chapter

Week 4: Lifestyle Embedding

- Assess what's working and what needs adjustment
- Plan for month 2 based on what you've learned about your actual patterns
- Celebrate the fact that you've built a month of creative consistency

Your 30-Day Integration Tracker:

Week 1 - Foundation:
- ☐ Identified primary block type: _____
- ☐ Chose main technique: _____
- ☐ Completed minimum daily practice: ___/7 days
- ☐ Notable patterns: _____

Week 2 - Environment:
- ☐ Space optimization completed
- ☐ Digital boundaries implemented
- ☐ Environment impact noticed: _____
- ☐ Daily practice maintained: ___/7 days

Week 3 - Integration:
- ☐ Secondary technique added: _____
- ☐ Tool combinations tried: _____
- ☐ Weekly review completed
- ☐ Daily practice maintained: ___/7 days

Week 4 - Lifestyle:
- ☐ What's working: _____
- ☐ What needs adjustment: _____
- ☐ Month 2 plan: _____
- ☐ Daily practice maintained: ___/7 days

Overall Assessment:

And The Mellow Mastermind Way To Fix It

```
Energy level change: _____
Confidence change: _____
Joy in creating change:
_____
Biggest insight:
_____
```

Remember: This Is a Practice, Not a Performance

The Mellow Mastermind lifestyle isn't a destination you arrive at and maintain perfectly forever. It's a way of approaching creativity that you practice, imperfectly, over time.

You'll have Mellow Mastermind days when everything flows and you remember why you love creating. You'll have decidedly non-mellow-mastermind days when you fall back into old patterns. Both are normal. Both are part of the journey.

The difference is that now you have tools. You have permission. You have a framework for working with your humanity instead of against it.

Most importantly, you have a new relationship with your creativity — one based on curiosity instead of pressure, sustainable practices instead of unsustainable sprints, and being human instead of being perfect.

The Compound Effect Promise:

If you apply even 50% of what you've learned in this book, consistently over the next six months, your creative life will be unrecognizable. Not because you'll become a different person, but because you'll become a more sustainable, confident, and joyful version of the creative person you already are.

The changes might be subtle at first:

- You'll notice you start creative work more easily
- Perfectionism will still show up, but you'll recognize it faster and have tools to work with it
- You'll finish more projects because you'll start more projects
- Your creative identity will feel more solid and less dependent on external validation
- Rest will feel like strategy instead of laziness

> *Your creative future is bright, sustainable, and entirely possible.*

You don't need to be perfect at being a Mellow Mastermind. You don't need to use every technique perfectly or maintain perfect consistency. You just need to keep showing up to your own creative life with the tools, permission, and self-compassion you've learned.

The blank page is waiting. Not for perfection — just for you to begin, again and again, with whatever energy and capacity you have today.

And The Mellow Mastermind Way To Fix It

Welcome to your new creative operating system. Time to see what you can build when you stop fighting yourself and start working with the beautiful, messy, perfectly imperfect human you are.

Why You're Creatively Blocked

Quick Reference Guide
Your Creative Emergency Toolkit

When you're in the middle of a creative crisis, you don't need inspiration. You need instructions.

This section is your creative first aid kit — quick diagnosis and immediate action steps for when your brain is being dramatic and you can't remember which chapter has the solution you need.

DO THIS NOW: THE CRISIS ASSESSMENT

Before diving into solutions, spend 30 seconds identifying what you're actually dealing with:

Time needed: 30 seconds

Read each statement and pick the ONE that makes you go "oh man, that's exactly what's happening right now":

☐ "I've been staring at this for 20 minutes and haven't started" ☐ "I keep tweaking the same thing over and over" ☐ "I can't focus for more than 2 minutes before getting distracted" ☐ "I have 47 ideas and can't decide which one to work on" ☐ "I used to love this, but now it feels like a chore"

Your answer determines which emergency protocol to use. Don't overthink it — go with your gut reaction.

Emergency Block Diagnosis (30 Seconds)

The Overthinking Spiral *"I need to research this more before I can possibly start"*

What it looks like:

- Stuck in planning mode for days/weeks
- Know more about your topic than actual experts
- Zero work produced despite hours of "preparation"
- Browser has 23 tabs open for "research"

Emergency Response: 5-Minute Creation Override

The Perfectionist Freeze *"I can't share this until it's completely perfect"*

What it looks like:

- Editing the same section for the 17th time
- Haven't posted anything in months because nothing feels "ready"
- Spend more time tweaking than creating new work
- Everything feels "almost done" but never actually gets finished

Emergency Response: 70% Ship-It Protocol

Why You're Creatively Blocked

The Distraction Tornado *"I'll definitely start after I just check one more thing"*

What it looks like:

- Somehow organizing Spotify playlists instead of working
- Phone buzzing constantly within arm's reach
- Can't maintain focus for more than 2-3 minutes
- "Just checking something quickly" becomes an hour-long scroll session

Emergency Response: Digital Detox + Environment Control

The Idea-Hopping Chaos *"But this new idea is so much more exciting than what I was working on"*

What it looks like:

- Multiple brilliant unfinished projects
- Get excited about new concepts, bored with current ones
- Haven't completed anything substantial in months
- Feel guilty about abandoned projects but keep starting new ones

Emergency Response: One-Project Lockdown

And The Mellow Mastermind Way To Fix It

The Burnout Shutdown *"I used to love this, but now it feels like another obligation"*

What it looks like:

- Exhaustion that sleep doesn't fix
- Resentment toward your creative practice
- Everything feels like work, nothing feels like play
- Creating feels like another item on an impossible to-do list

Emergency Response: STOP. Rest Protocol Activated

Creative Emergency Protocols

> ### Protocol 1: Complete Creative Paralysis
>
> *"I'm completely stuck and can't even start"*
>
> Time needed: 5 minutes maximum
>
> **Immediate Actions:**
>
> 1. **Set phone timer for 5 minutes** (not phone timer — use a physical one if possible)
> 2. **Do LITERALLY anything related to your project:**
>   - Open the document and type one word
>   - Draw one squiggly line on paper

Why You're Creatively Blocked

- - - Record 10 seconds of humming a melody
    - Take one photo of something related to your idea
    - Write your project title in terrible handwriting
3. **When the timer goes off:** You can stop OR keep going (no pressure either way)
4. **If you stopped:** Celebrate showing up — that was the whole goal
5. **If you continued:** You just successfully tricked your brain

If that didn't work: Change location completely. Take your materials to your car, a tea shop, outside, anywhere that's not where you usually try to work.

Protocol 2: Creative Overwhelm

"There's too much to do and I don't know where to start"

Time needed: 10 minutes total

Phase 1: Brain Dump (5 minutes)

- Write EVERYTHING you're thinking about on paper
- Don't organize, categorize, or prioritize — just empty your head

- Include creative projects, life tasks, random worries, everything
- Keep writing until the timer goes off, even if you repeat things

Phase 2: Micro-Focus (5 minutes)

1. **Circle ONE thing** from your brain dump that you could make progress on today
2. **Make it smaller:** What's the tiniest version of that thing you could do right now?
3. **Do only that micro-version** for 15 minutes maximum
4. **Stop when the timer goes off** (even if you want to continue)
5. **Tomorrow:** Pick the next smallest thing from your list

Emergency Mantras:

- "I don't have to do everything. I just have to do something."
- "Progress is progress, regardless of size."
- "One small step is infinitely better than zero steps."

Protocol 3: Perfectionist Spiral

Why You're Creatively Blocked

"This isn't good enough and I can't stop tweaking it"

Time needed: Immediate action required

Emergency Shutdown:

1. **Set deadline for TODAY** (yes, today — not tomorrow, not this weekend)
2. **Define "good enough"**: Ask only "Does this solve the problem it set out to solve?" If yes, proceed to step 3
3. **Ship whatever exists when the deadline hits** (no exceptions, no "just one more thing")
4. **Before you ship**: Write down one thing you learned from making this
5. **After you ship**: Immediately do something physical — walk, stretch, clean something
6. **Don't check responses** for at least 4 hours (set another timer for this)

Emergency Mantras:

- "Done is better than perfect, and perfect is usually just another word for never."
- "This is good enough to help someone. That's all it needs to be."

And The Mellow Mastermind Way To Fix It

> - "I can always make something better after I've made something."

Protocol 4: Focus Hijacking

"I can't concentrate for more than 30 seconds"

Time needed: 2 minutes setup, then focused work cycles

Immediate Environment Control:

1. **Phone in airplane mode** (not just silent — airplane mode)
2. **Physical timer** (never use phone timer when focusing)
3. **One task only** (close all other tabs, put away other projects, clear desk surface)
4. **Remove visual distractions** (face away from windows, cover mirrors, clear desk)

Focus Building Sequence:

- **Round 1:** 15 minutes of work, 5 minutes of break
- **Round 2:** 20 minutes of work, 5 minutes of break

Why You're Creatively Blocked

- **Round 3:** 25 minutes of work, longer break

Check phone only during designated breaks

If you can't even handle airplane mode:

- Put phone in different room
- If that's impossible, put it in a drawer
- If that's impossible, put it face down with something heavy on top
- If that's impossible, delete the most distracting apps temporarily

Protocol 5: Creative Burnout

"I feel exhausted by the thought of creating anything"

Time needed: As long as it takes (this is not negotiable)

STOP. Do not pass go. Do not try to productivity-hack your way out of this.

Immediate Burnout Response:

1. **Acknowledge the reality:** "I am burned out, not blocked. These require different solutions."

2. **Give yourself permission** to rest without earning it or setting a timeline
3. **Set protective boundaries**: What will you NOT do this week to protect your recovery?
4. **Engage in actual restoration**: Sleep, nature, baths, fiction books, gentle movement, conversations with friends
5. **Avoid "productive rest"**: No creative podcasts, no planning your comeback, no organizing creative materials

Return Protocol:

- **Only return when genuinely excited** about creating again (not guilty-excited or should-excited)
- **Start with 5-minute sessions** and rebuild gradually
- **Monitor energy levels** — if creating drains rather than energizes, return to rest

Emergency Mantras:

- "Rest is not a reward I have to earn. It's maintenance I need to function."
- "Burnout is information, not failure."
- "I am more than my creative output."

The Decision Tree: Which Protocol When?

Use this flowchart when you're too overwhelmed to think clearly:

Start here: How is your energy level right now?

- Depleted/Exhausted (1-3/10) → Protocol 5 (Burnout) or rest first
- Low but functional (4-6/10) → Continue to next question
- Good energy (7-10/10) → Continue to next question

Next: What's your main obstacle right now?

- Can't start anything → Protocol 1 (Paralysis)
- Too many options/tasks → Protocol 2 (Overwhelm)
- Can't stop tweaking/perfecting → Protocol 3 (Perfectionist)
- Can't focus/keep getting distracted → Protocol 4 (Focus)
- Don't want to do any creative work → Protocol 5 (Burnout)

Finally: How long has this been going on?

- Today/this week → Use indicated protocol
- Multiple weeks → Consider deeper work with relevant chapter
- Multiple months → May need professional support or extended Chapter 7 protocols

And The Mellow Mastermind Way To Fix It

Quick Decision Flowchart Visual:

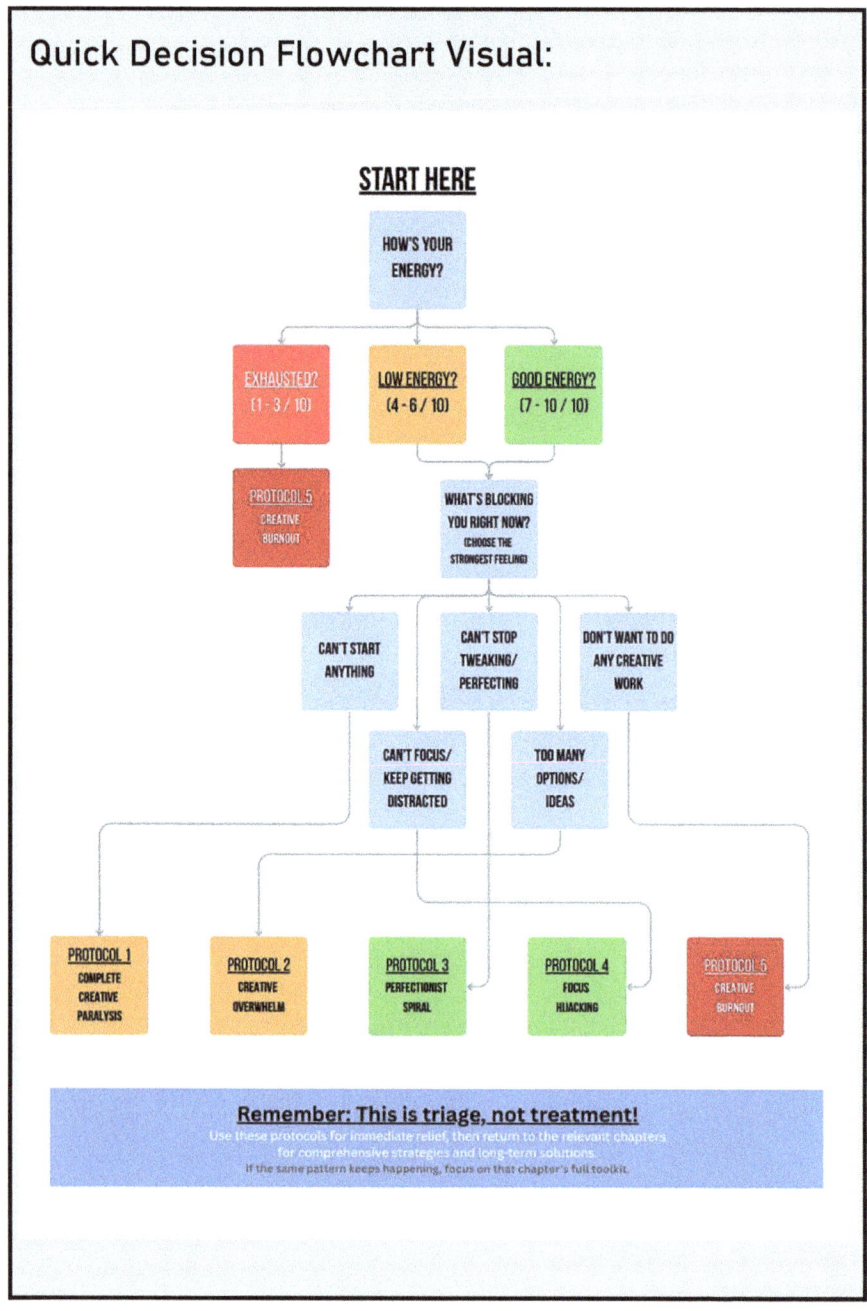

Daily Creative Survival Kit

> ### Morning Creative Activation (3 minutes)
>
> **Energy Check (30 seconds):** Rate your creative energy: ___/10 No judgment — just data about what you're working with today.
>
> **Permission Setting (60 seconds):** Complete this sentence: "Today I give myself permission to _____" Examples: "be terrible at this," "work for only 20 minutes," "experiment with no goal," "rest if I need to"
>
> **Micro-Commitment (90 seconds):** What's the smallest creative thing you could do today that would feel like a win? Write it down. Make it so small it feels almost silly not to do it.

> ### Resistance Response Protocol
>
> **When resistance hits during your creative session:**
>
> 1. **Name it specifically:** "I notice I'm feeling [exact emotion] about [specific task]"
>   - Not: "I'm feeling weird about this"

And The Mellow Mastermind Way To Fix It

- o Yes: "I'm feeling scared about sharing this poem"
2. **Shrink the task:** What's a smaller version you could do right now?
    - o Not: "Write the whole thing"
    - o Yes: "Write one terrible sentence"
3. **Start the timer:** 5 minutes, anything counts, begin now
4. **Celebrate the attempt:** You showed up — that's literally the entire game

---

End-of-Day Wind-Down (2 minutes)

Completion Celebration (30 seconds): Acknowledge that you honored your creative commitment, even if messily. The goal was showing up, not perfection.

Pattern Noting (60 seconds): What worked today? (Time, environment, approach, energy level) What felt sticky? (Not "what was bad" — what felt resistant or difficult)

Tomorrow Setup (30 seconds): Leave one breadcrumb for tomorrow's self. Open document, write next line, set up materials — something that makes starting easier.

Weekly Creative Maintenance (10 minutes every Sunday)

The Four Essential Questions:

1. What worked well this week? Not what was perfect — what actually functioned, felt good, or moved you forward.
2. What felt sticky or difficult?
   Not what was terrible — what patterns of resistance showed up repeatedly.
3. What did I learn about my creative process? About timing, environment, energy management, or effective approaches.
4. What wants to be explored next week? Stay curious rather than prescriptive. What feels alive or interesting to try?

Weekly Adjustment Protocol:

- If same block pattern showed up 3+ times: Focus on that chapter's techniques next week
- If energy was consistently low: Review Chapter 7 (rest and sustainability)
- If environment felt chaotic: Implement one Chapter 5 strategy
- If nothing got finished: Emphasize Chapter 3 (70% Rule) practices
- If joy was consistently low: Return to Chapter 2 (reconnect with influences that inspire)

Creative First Aid Mantras

Keep these saved in your phone for emergency use:

When you're stuck: "I don't need the perfect idea. I need the next small step."

When you're scared: "Courage isn't fearlessness. It's feeling scared and starting anyway."

When you're comparing: "I'm not competing with anyone. I'm becoming who I'm meant to be."

When you're wanting to be perfect:
"Done is better than perfect. Perfect is usually just another word for never."

When you're overwhelmed: "I don't have to do everything. I just have to do something."

When you're burned out: "Rest is not a reward. It's a requirement for sustainable creativity."

When you're starting: "I don't need to be ready. I just need to begin."

When you're sharing: "This is good enough to help someone. That's all it needs to be."

When you're doubting: "My worth isn't determined by my output. I am more than what I make."

When you're impatient: "I'm playing the long game. Consistency beats intensity every single time."

The Nuclear Options: When Nothing Else Works

These are pattern interruptions for when your usual strategies fail:

The Location Switch: Work somewhere you've never worked before. Library, tea shop, park bench, your car, a friend's house.

The Medium Switch: If you're a writer, try drawing your ideas. If you're visual, try writing about your concepts. If you work digitally, go analog.

The Collaboration Call: Text a creative friend: "I'm stuck on [specific project]. Want to brainstorm for 15 minutes?"

The Teaching Test: Explain your project to someone who knows nothing about it. If you can't explain it simply, you probably need to clarify your own thinking first.

The Opposite Day: Do the exact opposite of your usual approach. If you plan everything, try pure improvisation. If you wing it, try detailed outlining.

The Deadline Fake-Out: Tell someone you'll send them your work by end of day (even if it's rough). Nothing motivates like external accountability.

The Constraint Game: Give yourself an artificial limitation: Write using only words that start with 'S', design using only three colors, compose using only four chords.

Emergency Contact List

When you need community:

- Discord Servers: Search "[your creative field] + Discord" or "Mellow Mastermind Community Server" for active communities
- Local Groups: Meetup.com for in-person creative groups in your area

When you need inspiration:

- Creative Live: Free classes across multiple creative disciplines
- YouTube: Search "creative process + [your medium]" for behind-the-scenes content

When you need technical help:

- YouTube University: Free tutorials for any creative skill
- Local Library: Most have free access to creative software and classes

When you need mental health support:

- Crisis Text Line: Text HOME to 741741 (US)
- BetterHelp: Online therapy platform
- Psychology Today: Find local therapists who understand creative challenges

Keep This Accessible

Screenshot these sections for quick phone access:

- The 30-second block diagnosis
- Your specific emergency protocol
- The resistance response steps
- The mantra that works best for your brain

Print and keep nearby:

- Daily survival kit checklist
- Weekly maintenance questions
- Decision tree flowchart

Save to your home screen:

- One mantra that consistently helps you
- Emergency contact info for your creative support people
- Link to this guide in your notes app

Final Reality Check

Remember: You're not broken. Your creative process isn't broken. You're just human, dealing with the very human challenge of bringing ideas into reality.

The goal is not to never struggle. The goal is to struggle more skillfully, with better tools, and way more self-

compassion than you probably think you deserve (but absolutely do).

You've got this. Not because you're perfect, but because you're persistent. Not because it's easy, but because it matters to you enough to keep showing up.

Now go make something. Even if it's terrible. Especially if it's terrible.

The world needs your version of imperfect more than it needs your version of perfect.

For deeper work on any of these emergency situations, return to the relevant chapter for comprehensive strategies and long-term solutions. This guide is your first aid kit — the chapters are your comprehensive treatment plan.

Why You're Creatively Blocked

Resources and Tools for the Mellow Mastermind

Your Curated Toolkit for Creative Unblocking and Sustainable Productivity

Before we dive into specific recommendations, let's establish some ground rules about tools and the Mellow Mastermind philosophy.

You don't need every tool on this list. You probably don't need most of them. What you need are the specific tools that work with your creative style, your budget, and your actual (not aspirational) creative habits.

> ### DO THIS NOW: THE TOOL AUDIT REALITY CHECK
>
> Before adding any new tools to your creative life, let's get honest about what you're actually working with:
>
> Time needed: 3 minutes
>
> 1. List the creative tools you currently own but don't use: (Apps on your phone, supplies in drawers, subscriptions you forgot about)
> 2. Identify your "productivity graveyard": What systems have you tried and abandoned in the past year?

> 3. **Rate your current tool satisfaction:** On a scale of 1-10, how well do your existing tools actually serve your creative process?
> 4. **Define your tool personality:** Are you a minimalist (fewer, better tools) or a maximalist (lots of options for different moods)?
> 5. **Set your tool budget:** How much are you willing to spend monthly on creative tools? ($0, $1-10, $10-50, $50+)
>
> Keep these answers visible as you read this chapter. They'll help you choose tools that actually fit your life instead of the life you think you should have.

The Mellow Mastermind Tool Selection Philosophy

The Reality Check Principle

I use maybe six tools from this entire list regularly. My actual daily toolkit: Pandora, Voice Memos, generic pens, a generic laptop stand, noise-canceling headphones, and Headspace. That's it. Everything else is experimental, situational, or recommended based on other people's success.

The Three-Tool Rule

Start with maximum three new tools at once. Master those before adding more. Too many new systems create decision fatigue and setup friction that kills creative momentum.

The 5-Minute Setup Test

If a tool takes more than 5 minutes to set up and start using, it might be too complex for daily creative practice. Simplicity wins over features every time.

The Weekly Tool Audit

Every Sunday, ask: "Which tools helped my creativity this week? Which created more work than value?" Eliminate ruthlessly based on actual use, not theoretical utility.

Tool Selection Framework:

Before adding any new tool, ask:

☐ Does this solve a specific problem I actually have?
☐ Can I start using it effectively within 5 minutes?
☐ Will this simplify or complicate my creative process?
☐ Am I buying this tool or buying the fantasy of who I'll become?
☐ Do I have budget/energy to learn this properly?

Essential Apps & Digital Tools

Writing & Ideation

Obsidian (Free/Premium) *The connected thinking workspace*

Pricing accurate as of 2025 – check current rates as these change frequently

Best for: People who think in networks rather than linear lists

- Daily notes for capturing creative fragments without pressure
- Graph view reveals unexpected connections between ideas
- Perfect for the "remix method" from Chapter 2

When to choose this: You have lots of scattered ideas and want to see how they connect

When to skip this: You prefer simple, linear organization.

Notion (Free/Premium) *The all-in-one workspace that adapts to your brain*

Pricing accurate as of 2025 – check current rates as these change frequently

Best for: People who want one tool for everything

- Template gallery includes creative project management
- Database features help track creative wins without spreadsheet nightmare
- Flexible enough to grow with your changing needs

When to choose this: You're tired of juggling multiple apps and want one flexible system

When to skip this: You get overwhelmed by too many features or prefer specialized tools

---

Voice Memos (Built into most phones) *The ultimate friction-free capture tool*

Best for: Everyone (seriously, everyone needs this)

- Perfect for shower thoughts and commute ideas
- Zero setup required = no excuses for not capturing ideas
- Works with any creative medium (record melodies, describe visual concepts, ramble through problems)

When to choose this: You're human with ideas that happen at inconvenient times

When to skip this: Never skip this — it's free and already on your phone.

And The Mellow Mastermind Way To Fix It

Focus & Time Management

Forest (Premium - ~$4) *Gamified focus sessions without productivity shame*

Pricing accurate as of 2025 - check current rates as these change frequently

Best for: People motivated by visual progress and gentle accountability

- Plant virtual trees during creative sessions (surprisingly satisfying)
- Community features connect you with other humans trying to focus
- Cute enough to feel like play rather than work

When to choose this: You need focus help but productivity apps usually stress you out

When to skip this: You're motivated by data/metrics rather than visual rewards.

Freedom (Premium - ~$3-8/month) *Website and app blocker for protecting creative time*

Pricing accurate as of 2025 - check current rates as these change frequently

Best for: People with serious digital distraction issues

- Schedule blocks during deep work sessions

- Reveals exactly how much time you lose to scrolling (prepare to be humbled)
- Can block specific sites or categories across all devices

When to choose this: You consistently lose creative time to digital distractions

When to skip this: You can manage distractions with simpler methods (airplane mode, etc.)

Physical Tools & Supplies

The Anti-Perfectionist Desk Setup

Pilot G2 Pens (~$2-15 for multi-packs) *The reliable creative companion*

Pricing accurate as of 2025 - check current rates as these change frequently

Why these specifically:

- Smooth writing that doesn't interrupt creative flow
- Available everywhere (no excuse for not having one)
- Multiple colors for different types of thinking
- Cheap enough to buy in bulk and scatter everywhere

Rhodia Notebooks (~$8-25) *High-quality paper without preciousness*

Pricing accurate as of 2025 - check current rates as these change frequently

Why these work:

- Paper quality makes writing feel special without being too nice to use
- Dot grid format works for both writing and sketching
- Multiple sizes for different contexts and energy levels
- Durable enough for daily creative abuse

When to choose these: You want a physical notebook that feels good but not too precious

When to skip these: Any notebook works — these are a nice-to-have, not essential

---

Adjustable Laptop Stand (~$25-80) *Ergonomics that enable longer creative sessions*

Pricing accurate as of 2025 – check current rates as these change frequently

Why this matters:

- Reduces neck strain during longer creative work
- Creates visual separation between "work mode" and "create mode"
- Easier to shift between standing and sitting when you get antsy
- Makes any space feel more like an intentional workspace

Noise-Canceling Headphones (~$100-350) *Investment in creative boundaries*

Pricing accurate as of 2025 - check current rates as these change frequently

Why these are worth it:

- Essential for creating boundaries in shared spaces
- Works with whatever music helps your brain focus
- Signals to others (and yourself) that you're in creative mode
- Reduces decision fatigue about where to work

When to invest: You work in noisy environments or need clear creative boundaries

Budget alternatives: Any headphones + focus music, earplugs, white noise apps

---

The Grab-and-Go Creative Kit

Small Waterproof Bag (~$10-30) *Portable creative readiness*

Pricing accurate as of 2025 - check current rates as these change frequently

What goes in it:

- Pens that definitely work
- Small notebook or index cards
- Phone charger (because dead phones kill creativity)

- Business cards or contact info for creative connections
- One inspiring object (photo, quote, small artwork)

Why this matters: Removes setup friction so you can create anywhere inspiration strikes

Index Cards (~$3-8) *Physical idea manipulation*

Pricing accurate as of 2025 - check current rates as these change frequently

Why these specifically:

- Perfect size for brain dumps when digital feels overwhelming
- Physical manipulation helps with idea sorting and organizing
- Works when your phone is dead or distracting
- Cheap enough to use freely without being precious

Creative Applications:

- One idea per card for easy sorting and reorganization
- Story/project planning with moveable scenes or concepts
- Daily intention cards (shuffle and pick one)
- Gratitude or win-tracking that feels less formal than journaling

Music & Audio for Creative Focus

Brain.fm (Premium - ~$7/month) *Music designed for cognitive states*

Pricing accurate as of 2025 - check current rates as these change frequently

Why this works:

- Different modes for different types of creative work
- Scientifically designed to influence brainwaves
- No lyrics or sudden changes to break flow

When to invest: You're serious about focus and willing to pay for effectiveness

Budget alternative: Spotify focus playlists (free but less targeted)

Spotify Focus Playlists (Free with ads/Premium) *Curated background music*

Pricing accurate as of 2025 - check current rates as these change frequently

Best playlists:

- "Deep Focus" - electronic music designed for concentration
- "Peaceful Piano" - instrumental without emotional distraction

- "Ambient Relaxation" - atmospheric sounds for gentle focus

Pro tip: Create your own based on what actually helps your specific brain focus

Nature Sounds & White Noise *Consistent background without distraction*

Best apps: Noisli, A Soft Murmur, or simple YouTube videos
Why this works: Masks distracting environmental sounds without adding musical distraction

---

Budget-Conscious Tool Recommendations

Pricing accurate as of 2025 - check current rates as these change frequently

Free Tier Recommendations

Essential tools that work without paid upgrades:

- Voice Memos (built-in)
- Any basic notes app
- YouTube for learning
- Library resources (often include creative software access)
- Free meditation apps
- Spotify free for focus music

Under $25 Investment

Tools worth the small investment:

- Good pens and basic notebook
- Phone stand or laptop stand
- Index cards for physical idea manipulation
- One month of a premium app to test if it's worth ongoing cost

$25-100 Investment

Tools that significantly improve creative infrastructure:

- Decent headphones (doesn't have to be top-of-line)
- Ergonomic workspace improvements
- One high-quality creative software subscription
- Physical creative supplies specific to your medium

$100+ Investment

Only invest here after establishing consistent creative practice:

- Professional software subscriptions
- High-end equipment specific to your creative field
- Courses or coaching
- Premium workspace solutions

```
Budget Planning Template:

My monthly creative tool budget:
$_____

Current tool expenses: $_____

Tools I want to try:
_____

Priority order: 1._____ 2._____
3._____

Test period plan:
_____

Success metrics:
_____
```

The Anti-Productivity-Addiction Protocol

Warning Signs You've Gone Too Far:

- Spend more time optimizing tools than using them
- Have multiple unused subscriptions for similar services
- Constantly search for "better" tools instead of mastering current ones
- Feel anxiety when you can't access your perfect setup
- Tools have become more complex than the creative work itself

Tool Detox Protocol:

1. List all your creative tools (apps, subscriptions, physical supplies)
2. Identify what you actually used this month
3. Cancel/remove anything unused for 30+ days
4. Choose 3 tools maximum for the next month
5. Track satisfaction weekly - do these tools help or hinder?

Sustainable Tool Habits:

- Monthly tool review: Keep only what serves your actual creative practice
- One-in-one-out rule: Before adding new tools, remove old ones
- Function over features: Choose tools based on what you need, not what's impressive
- Regular simplification: Periodically reduce to bare essentials to reset perspective

---

Your Personal Tool Selection Plan

> **Complete Tool Selection Worksheet:**
>
> **Step 1: Current State Assessment**
>
> Creative tools I currently use regularly:
> _____
> _____

And The Mellow Mastermind Way To Fix It

```
Tools I own but don't use:
_____

Monthly cost of current tools:
$_____

Satisfaction with current setup (1-10):
_____
```

Step 2: Specific Need Identification

```
My biggest creative challenge:
_____
_____

Tool category that might help:
_____
_____

Specific problem to solve:
_____

Budget for solution:
$_____
```

Step 3: Implementation Plan

```
Tool to try first:
_____

Test period length:
_____
```

```
Success criteria:
_____

Backup plan if it doesn't work:
_____

Step 4: Integration Strategy

Which chapter's techniques will this
support: _____

How will I measure if it's working:
_____
_____

When will I evaluate and decide to
keep/remove:
_____
```

Final Reality Check: Tools Serve Creativity, Not the Reverse

Remember: Your creative practice is about creating, not optimizing. These tools exist to support that creating, never to replace the fundamental work of showing up and making things.

> **The most important tool in your creative toolkit will always be your willingness to start before you're ready and share before you're perfect.**

Everything else is just helpful support for that fundamental creative courage.

And The Mellow Mastermind Way To Fix It

Tools won't make you creative. They can only remove friction from the creativity you already have. Choose tools that serve your creative process, not ones that promise to transform you into someone else.

Start small. Stay consistent. Let your toolkit grow organically as your creative practice evolves.

For personalized guidance on building systems that work with your specific creative blocks and patterns, the Mellow Mastermind Workbook transforms these general recommendations into customized strategies for your unique creative journey.

P.S. - If you work for any of the companies mentioned above and want to discuss partnership opportunities, I'm professionally enthusiastic about products I actually use and recommend. My DMs are appropriately open.

Get To Know the Author

Wanda Rogers is a creative professional who understands the particular brand of chaos that comes with being multi-passionate in a world that demands specialization.

> If this book resonated with you, you're not alone in your creative journey. Take 2 minutes to:
>
> 1. Follow @MellowMastermind on Instagram, YouTube, or TikTok for ongoing creative support
> 2. Visit www.officiallymars.com to access free resources and community updates
> 3. Share one insight from this book with another creative person in your life
> 4. Tag your creative wins with #MellowMastermind so others can celebrate with you
>
> Building creative community is just as important as building creative skills.

By day, Wanda works in IT — solving problems, managing systems, and keeping technology running smoothly. By night (and early morning, and lunch breaks, and honestly whenever inspiration strikes), she's a music artist who sings, produces beats, writes poetry, and mentors fellow creatives through their own creative blocks.

Based in Texas but forever carrying her Florida roots, Wanda has spent over two decades navigating the creative landscape as someone who refuses to pick just one artistic lane. She's been singing since she was three years old and making music since she was around twelve, which means she's had plenty of time to perfect every possible form of creative procrastination known to humanity.

This book was born from Wanda's own epic battles with creative paralysis — particularly the kind that happens when you have seventeen brilliant ideas and can't figure out which one deserves your attention... or when you're terrified to share your work because what if people think it's terrible?

After years of helping friends, family, and fellow creators work through their own creative resistance patterns, she realized that most productivity advice treats symptoms rather than root causes. The breakthrough came when she stopped trying to fix her "broken" creative brain and started designing systems that worked with her natural chaos instead of against it.

Wanda's approach to creativity is refreshingly honest about the messy reality of creative life:

- She's a recovering perfectionist who learned that strategic rest is more productive than forcing inspiration
- She's a proudly distracted mastermind who discovered that working with your brain's natural chaos is more effective than fighting it
- She's a multi-passionate creator who believes your diverse interests are a strategic advantage, not a character flaw
- Most importantly, she's someone who believes your creative practice should energize your life, not consume it

Her philosophy centers on what she calls "strategic humanity" — building creative systems that honor both your ambition and your actual human limitations. This means working with your natural rhythms instead of against them, giving yourself permission to create imperfectly, and understanding that sustainable creativity is built through consistency, not intensity.

As a mentor and speaker, Wanda has helped hundreds of creators move from creative paralysis to consistent creative action. Her approach combines practical productivity strategies with the psychological insights needed to address why we avoid our creative work in the first place.

Common transformations from her mentoring work:

- Writers who went from "someday I'll write a book" to actually finishing what they've started
- Musicians who stopped perfecting bedroom recordings and started sharing their work
- Visual artists who overcame impostor syndrome and launched their first shows
- Entrepreneurs who built sustainable creative businesses without burning out

She's particularly passionate about helping multi-passionate creatives stop apologizing for their diverse interests and start leveraging their creative breadth as a strategic advantage.

And The Mellow Mastermind Way To Fix It

Beyond the Book: Current Creative Projects

The Mellow Mastermind Workbook: A companion guide that transforms the principles in this book into personalized creative systems tailored to your specific block patterns and creative goals.

Corporate Creativity Training: Workshops for teams and organizations that want to foster sustainable innovation without contributing to employee burnout.

Individual Creative Coaching: One-on-one mentoring for creators ready to build long-term creative practices that serve their whole lives, not just their creative output.

Music Under @OfficiallyMars: Where she practices what she preaches about shipping work at 70% and remixing influences from across genres and decades.

When she's not making music, writing, or helping other creatives get unstuck, you can find Wanda enjoying life with the people she cares about, probably taking a strategically timed nap that will somehow lead to her next creative breakthrough, or reorganizing her creative workspace to include her favorite snacks and drinks.

Wanda's real education has come from two decades of creative experimentation, strategic failure, and learning to work with her beautifully chaotic creative brain instead of against it.

Connect with the Mellow Mastermind Community:

Website: www.officiallymars.com
Community: @MellowMastermind on Instagram, YouTube, TikTok, and the 'Mellow Mastermind Community Server' on Discord
Speaking: Available for workshops, corporate creativity training, and conferences
Music: @OfficiallyMars on all streaming platforms

Quick Reference: How to Stay Connected

☐ Weekly Creative Tips: Follow @MellowMastermind for bite-sized strategies
☐ Deep Dive Content: Subscribe to the newsletter at officiallymars.com
☐ Community Support: Join discussions using #MellowMastermind
☐ Workshop Updates: Check the speaking calendar for events near you
☐ Personal Coaching: Apply through the website for one-on-one mentoring

And The Mellow Mastermind Way To Fix It

A Note from Wanda:

> *"The goal isn't to become a perfect creator. The goal is to become a consistent one. Everything else is just extra details."*

If this book helped you get unstuck, create something you're proud of, or simply gave you permission to rest without guilt, I'd love to hear about it. The creative journey can feel isolating, but you're not alone in this. We're all figuring it out as we go along — the difference is having better tools and more self-compassion for the journey.

Your creative work matters! Not because it has to be perfect, not because it has to change the world, but because it's yours. Because you showed up. Because you chose creation over consumption, courage over comfort, and progress over perfection.

Keep creating, keep experimenting, and remember: your brain isn't broken. You just needed a better manual.

For media inquiries, speaking requests, or collaboration opportunities, contact through info@officiallymars.com

---

www.ingramcontent.com/pod-product-compliance
Lightning Source LLC
Chambersburg PA
CBHW050927240426
43670CB00023B/2962